The Recipe for Sticky Customers

The secret to forever fans for every small business

Janet Wentworth

The 10X Group | Santa Rosa, California

10X group

The Recipe for Sticky Customers: The secret to forever fans for any small business

Published by:

The 10X Group
725 College Avenue, Suite 1
Santa Rosa, CA 95404

Email: janet.wentworth@gmail.com
www.unstoppablebrand.com
Unstoppable Brand™ of Janet Wentworth

First published in 2017

ISBN: 978-0-9895309-2-7

Printed in the United States of America

DISCLAIMER

This book is designed to provide small business owners with a process and ideas to improve their marketing by using business stories and emotional branding. Topics covered are not exhaustive but are designed to supplement existing resources. The author and publisher make no representations or warranties and assume no liabilities of any kind with the respect to the accuracy or completeness of the content of this book or its suitability for any particular business. Unless otherwise specifically stated, the views are those of the author. Readers assume responsibility for their use of the information and ideas presented.

Preface

Are you trying to crack the code to attracting the right customers and keeping them coming back for more?

Are you envious of the rabid fans of Apple, Harley Davidson or Tesla —and feel you could never do the same?

You may moan about your lack of money to market yourself. But a big budget is no guarantee of success. Ask Coke about their failed introduction of New Coke. Or Ford Motor Company about the Edsel. It isn't about having the best product or service. It isn't about your price. It isn't about your Facebook page.

Success is not based on the traditional four pillars of marketing-- your mix of product, price, position and promotion. So what does determine success?

The secret is understanding how to create emotional connections with your ideal customers. These emotional connections create brand zealots for Nike, Star Trek, or even the local taco truck. You can create the same customer stickiness regardless of what you sell, the size of your budget, or your marketing experience.

In The Recipe for Sticky Customers we explore:

- the 6 critical elements of building a sticky brand

- how these elements work together to create an emotional glue

- why it's true that people buy on emotion and justify on facts

- the real definition of "story" that will make all the difference in how you use this proven powerful method of persuasion

- how to create your unique recipe for sticky customers

Worried that you are already overwhelmed with no time to add more to your plate? Let me give you another secret: it isn't about doing more. Even time-challenged business owners will learn that it is about doing what you do with an awareness of your brand recipe.

During this you will work on Mind Maps for your brand elements and a roadmap for implementation. You will find you can start small and grow at your own pace. The only requirement is to come with a mind open to the possibilities of emotional connections for your customers. Regardless of the size of your business or your resources, you will discover ideas for creating sticky customers.

Janet Wentworth

Sticky Customers is another way of talking about branding.

But branding has a way of scaring small business owners. It reeks of jargon and mystery. Books and articles tout why you need to create engaging experiences and delight your customer, but they offer scant information on HOW to do this. And they never mention the reality of small budgets and few other resources.

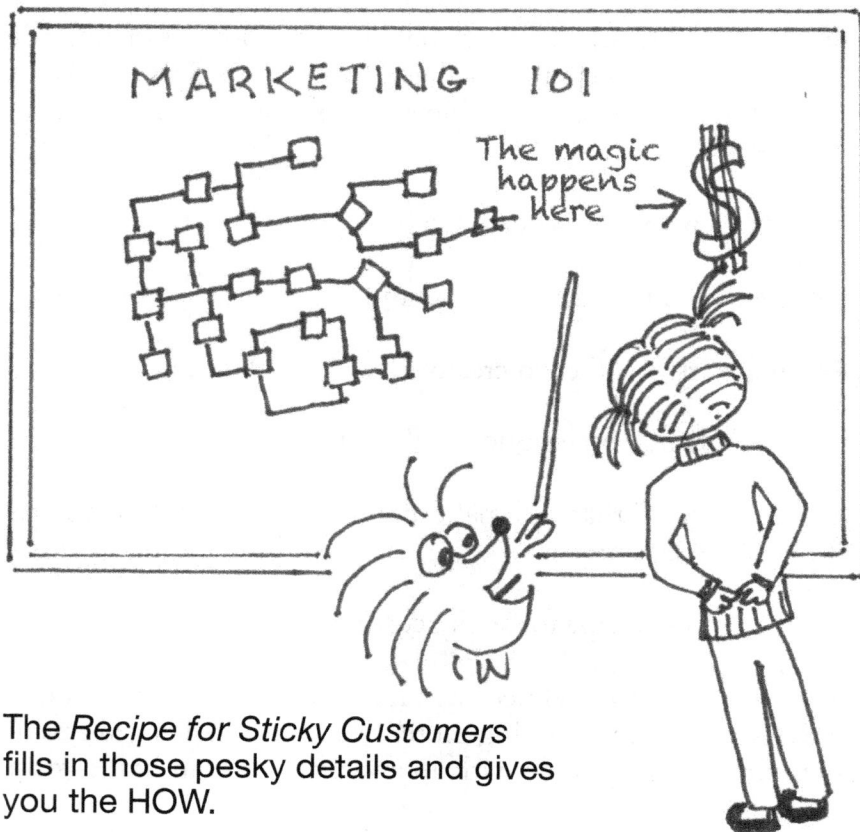

MARKETING 101

The magic happens here →

The *Recipe for Sticky Customers* fills in those pesky details and gives you the HOW.

Contents

What Are Sticky Customers?

Sticky customers are those customers who love what you do. They like you and trust you. They are loyal and return for more of what you offer. They tell their friends. They leave great reviews on Yelp and other consumer review sites. Maybe they have written a Facebook post about you or feature your products in their Instagram feed. They give you useful feedback. They will pay a higher price or go out of their way to visit you because they love the experience and want to support you. They want you to succeed.

These are the people that make your business a success. And more than that, their support feeds your passion. Because of them you know what you doing is needed and loved. It stokes your inner fire to keep going even in the face of new competition, economic shifts and the struggle to find employees who share your passion. You know what you do is worthwhile and you know it is important to your customers.

Having sticky customers is a game changer. You are no longer beaten down by wave after wave of challenges; you are riding a wave of customer love.

Branding —What Is It?

OK. There I have said it. The B word. I usually try to avoid using this word because it is used so frequently and yet so misunderstood.

Some people think branding is coming up with a logo. Others think is some evil plot to manipulate consumers. Some believe it is so complicated and expensive only "big brands" can develop a brand. Others are just too darn overwhelmed with everything they need to do that any thoughts of branding will just have to wait for that magical day when they have empty space on their to-do list.

This is all wrong-headed.

Every business has a brand (In fact, every person has a brand)

A brand is what a person thinks when they hear your name (where "your" can be you or your business). Notice I didn't say when "people" hear your name. Brand is personal.

Some people love Trader Joe's markets. They find them exciting, full of quirky, exotic food products, attention-grabbing chalkboard signs, happy employees and a great escape from the usual bland grocery store. But others find Trader Joe's annoying. From its rather eclectic mix of products to its usually cramped parking lots, visiting TJ's is can be an experience of fearing for your car's safety and leaving empty handed because you couldn't find the "regular stuff" that you needed. In the middle are those who just think "meh" when they hear the Trader Joe's name.

Each person is correct. And your job as a business owner is to understand your best customers, what delights them and offer them that experience in spades. Trader Joe's doesn't worry about those who would rather shop at Safeway or get their groceries by drone. They focus on giving more of what their best customers love about them.

You can never make everyone happy, so why try? Instead double down on the ones who share your values, love what you offer, and are delighted by the experience. **And all the work that is done to delight these people is called branding.**

The brand you want doesn't happen by chance.

Of course, creating an experience for your perfect customers with all the elements that are involved is a big project. And this is where many small business owners (and especially solo entrepreneurs) say, "No thanks. I just don't have the time."

That's OK. Let them go their way. But you are different. You understand that nurturing your brand is critical to your business success. Otherwise you wouldn't be reading this.

The good news is you can start with what you have and build a brand, one small step at a time. Apple began with 2 guys working in a garage and a hideous logo. (Google it if you don't believe me).

Apple grew. Added products. Developed whole new industries on its own. And along the way jettisoned that logo to become the powerhouse brand it is today.

You probably don't have the desire to be the next Apple. But you do want to attract your own tribe of loyal followers.

Worried About Being Overwhelmed? Don't be.

We are building a Minimum Viable Brand (MVB)

We will talk more about the MVB later. Just realize that our philosophy is (with thanks to tennis great Arthur Ashe):

Start where you are. Use what you have. Do what you can.

You start with whatever you have, even if it is only an idea. And you grow from there. But because you are using the MVB process you have a solid strategy. No just randomly trying things and hoping something works.

The Recipe for Sticky Customers can work with your schedule. It is best to work in order but if you are really stuck in one area, go ahead and move on to another. Sometimes you need to return to a previous topic because you realize you were on the wrong track or you have new ideas. That's OK. This isn't a race to the finish line, but it is important to get to the finish line. We will be covering a lot of territory, but everything is doable no matter how small your business or how crimped your budget.

Get started right now! Get a notebook so you can record all your assignments and thoughts in a single place. Ideas will start coming at the most inconvenient time, so be prepared. I even use AquaNotes which is a waterproof notebook that hangs on suction cups in my shower. That's where I get my best ideas and I know from experience, if I don't write them down right now, they are gone.

☑ **Assignment**

Begin by writing what you think people think/feel when they hear your name. What do you want people to think/feel when they hear your name? Is there a gap? Don't stew over this. Just put down your thoughts. Open your mind to possibilities.

"I've learned that people will forget what you said, people will forget what you did, but people will never forget how you made them feel."

Maya Angelou

Maya Angelou is not known as a branding expert but in this quotation she nailed it! And, if you follow the Recipe for Sticky Customers, you can nail it too.

Many people view branding as an exercise in creating logos, choosing colors, or packaging, signage and web page design.

These visual 2×4's are important but they aren't the whole building. And they only bring home the feeling you want to nurture if they are only intentionally, consistently and honestly employed

Brand is an emotional connection.

No single element makes a brand. It is carefully built, one strand at a time, like a tapestry. There are no shortcuts.

Your brand is built on the beliefs you share with your customers. You can't just have beliefs, you need to live them. Your Sticky Customer recipe is how to do this.

1. What you look like (ah, this is where that logo comes in.)

2. What you say.

3. What your rituals are.

4. What other sensory elements you use.

5. What you do.

And all of this results in how you make people feel.

These six ingredients (beliefs, look, say, rituals, sensory elements and actions) are what we will be covering in the remainder of this book.

Don't worry. It may sound overwhelming but it isn't. We will take one at a time and have plenty of time to reflect on each one and how it can apply to your business.

☑ Assignment

This is the start of your glue recipe. The glue that will create sticky customers.

In the first Assignment you were asked to think about what people feel when they hear your name. Now you should to think about any specific things that are cultivating this feeling. Jot down any ideas that come to you.

Often a brand will develop organically by the behavior of the owner and this leads to good things. But your brand can be so much stronger, those customers so much stickier, if you take that good foundation and hone and enlarge it intentionally and consistently.

Now it's time to get to work on creating that glue recipe you need for the business you want to build.

Your Glue Recipe

Every recipe has three components:

All recipes start with tools. Some are mental and some are physical.

Physical tools are things like bowls, frying pans, knives. We will not spend time on physical tools other then pen and paper to record your ideas. Once you get going you may need software to manipulate images or better quality paper for you promotional materials. What physical tools you need will come after you have created your recipe.

Mental tools are things like knowing how to fold egg whites into a souffle batter. Or how to debone a chicken or dice an onion.

Then comes the **list of ingredients.** The ingredients you choose are essential to the outcome you want. You can't randomly pull things off the pantry shelf and expect a great dish. Great food comes from balancing flavors, knowing how ingredients will interact, and how to choose for the best texture and visual appeal. How much salt is too much? Should you add salt to offset a bitterness? Will flake salt add a delightful crunch? You need to choose wisely.

And of course there is **the process.** How do you put these ingredients together to get the result you want? Even for the simple grilled cheese sandwich you need to make sure the cheese is between the bread slices and not the other way around!

Let's get started by discussing the five mental tools you need to create your Sticky Recipe.

Your Mental Tools

1. Target Customers/Your Vital Few

2. Emotions

3. Story

4. Journey Mindset

5. Possibilities Mindset

Tool #1 Your Vital Few

Vital Few may be a new term for you. The usual way to describe the customers you seek is target customer (or target audience).

The idea of a target customer is from the 1980's and the marketing-as-war mindset. It was quite popular thanks to the book Marketing Warfare by Al Ries and Jack Trout. The subtitle is "How American corporations are using military strategies to outmaneuver, outflank and even ambush their competition!"

If the subtitle isn't enough to get the message across, the cover has small tanks coming out of a briefcase to complete the visual.

I have yet to meet a small business owner or solopreneur who could warm up to the marketing-as-war philosophy.

These people are starting a business from a personal passion. An inner drive to do something good and yet still make money. They care about their customers and are willing to slog through the dark days of starting a business because of an inner fire.

Mostly, they are very open and welcoming. They see opportunities and look for partnerships.

The marketing-warfare types see a zero sum game: a dollar spent with a competitor is one dollar less for me.

When writing a marketing plan, writing about the customer as a target is uncomfortable.

Meet your Vital Few

Vital Few is a much better term. It allows for mutual benefit.

Vital Few sprang from the 80/20 Rule also known as the Pareto Principle. 80 percent of your revenue comes from 20 percent of your customers. Most people have heard of the 80/20 rule but few know that the original principle was the Vital Few and the Trivial Many. This is a much more useful way to think of your audience.

You are vital to me because you are my best customers, you buy often, and refer others.

I am vital to you because I offer what you need and listen to your suggestions.

It is a lovely symbiotic relationship. But what about the trivial many?

Too many small business owners try to reach everyone. It takes a leap of faith to realize that not everyone is right for what you offer. They may not need it. You may think you can help but they don't recognize they need help. They may already have a source they are happy with. They may not have enough money to buy it. They may not be motivated to make the commitment. They may see it as too risky.

You are better off ignoring these people, your Trivial Many. Just like the folks who don't like Trader Joes. Fine, let them go to Safeway. You have too many opportunities to create Sticky Customers with the ones who love you.

So who are your Vital Few?

If you already have a business, who are your best customers? The ones you wish you could clone?

If you are just starting and have few or no customers, you can ask friends or just go with your gut until you have started to attract customers.

Now start to define these people. Not just the standard demographics, like age, education, income level. But behaviors and values. What do they want their life to look like?

Ask yourself where they live, how they dress, where they go on vacation, what sort of car they drive. What wine club do they belong to, golf course do they play or campground to they visit? Each of these gives insights into the character of the person. The answers also show patterns of behavior and buying choices.

Become a Sherlock Holmes of reading people

Want to become a better customer detective? Read the blog post 9 Tips for Making Deductions Like Sherlock Holmes:
http://www.businessinsider.com/9-ways-to-observe-and-deduce-like-sherlock-holmes-2014-7

But also talk to them. People don't always give you the right answer. Not that they are lying to you, but that most of us don't even recognize why we do things! All of this observing and questioning is helping you form a very multi-dimensional snapshot of your best customers

You can read more about Vital Few here http://www.unstoppablebrand.com/forget-target-audience/

What is their inner goal that you are fulfilling?

Too often we focus on the thing we sell. We forget that we sell a product (or service) but they are buying to fill an emotional need.

A dentist may focus on her educational credentials, years of experience, professional staff. Many patients come for pain relief. But I may be buying self-esteem. I may want veneers to feed my vanity. Or those veneers may help quiet my story of being shamed for crooked teeth. Or I just want to feel empowered because I now earn a good salary and I can afford to do something expensive for myself.

When we choose a dentist it is for more than dental care. There is an inner reason that drives us to that dentist's reclining chair.

It is your job to know those inner desires of your Vital Few and offer to satisfy them.

✓ Assignment

Think about your Vital Few. Talk to people. Meditate. Do free writing. Or make a Mind Map. Take a shower or a walk. Do whatever helps you to open up to possibilities. This is best not done sitting at a computer. You need to open your mind. See what comes to you. Write it all down

Write a Letter from Your Customer. What would she say to you? Take the thoughts you have recorded and write from the heart. The Sample from Your Customer PDF on the next page may give you some ideas. This exercise can be the foundation of a stellar brand. It will give you the problems your customer is facing, the better future she desires, the words she uses, the places she can be found. In other words, this is the foundation of your marketing and branding.

Tool # 2 Emotions and Buying

Evolution has shaped how we think and feel.

We think of ourselves as a unified "self." We also like to think of ourselves as rational creatures. We do our research, analyze the choices, make a considered opinion.

Only this is not how it works. It is just the story we tell ourselves!

Our brains have evolved from our early reptile ancestors. Reptiles have only a brain stem that functions to control body systems (like breathing and heart rate) plus automatic response systems in place to worry about survival of self and survival of species. So we are wired to look for food, to keep breathing, to avoid danger. We are also wired for sex. All of these hard-wired systems keep us alive and propagating.

Letter from My Customer

What are her problems? Her hopes? The better future she wants? What are her beliefs? How does she see herself? How does she want others to see her? What happens in a typical day? What is the story she is telling herself? What story does she want to tell?

Your UNSTOPPABLE Brand

Recipe for Sticky Customers

As evolution continued, the mammal brain became larger and more complex. It began to process sensory information in new ways and developed memory and emotion. Mother Nature likes to keep things that work so mammals still have the original brain stem. After all it was a proven success. But continued evolution added processing that allows us to have emotional connections with all our sensory sensory inputs. This is our emotional brain.

But humans weren't finished evolving. On top of the brainstem and the emotional brain, humans developed an additional processing system that gave us language and analytic thought.

You can look at this as we have three brains. They are anatomically separate with defined functions but they are not totally independent.

An important point is that only the analytic brain has language. So it is of no use for your analytic brain to explain how many calories you have eaten today and that for your health you should not be eating those cookies. The emotional brain is all about how great they taste, and the aroma and memories of dipping those Oreos in milk as a kid. Guess what? Couple the lizard brain's goal of calories,with the emotional brain's memory of great taste and mom, and your rational brain in outnumbered and outmaneuvered.

An easy way to think of this is lizards have lust, dogs have loyalty and humans have romance.

But there is another interesting process in play here.

There is an old marketing saying "we buy on emotion and justify with facts." It seemed like a joke but recent science has proven this to be true.

Studies of people with damaged emotional brains (through injury or surgery) not only show little or no emotion they also have an extremely difficult time making decisions. It can take hours while the rational brain is deciding between the ham sandwich or the cheese. Or to even get up in the morning. It was clear that there was a connection between emotions and our decisions.

Now that functional MRI analysis of brain activity is a reality, scientists have been able to prove that when faced with making a decision, the emotional centers of a brain will light up with activity before the analytic brain becomes engaged.

Now we have proven that old saying to be accurate. And the marketer who relies only on data, facts and bullet points to make the sale will always lose to the savvy marketer who tells the story behind those analytic factors.

The takeaway for you? Embrace the fact that

- we buy (and make decisions in general) on emotion and then we justify with facts

- we buy from people we like and trust

- we buy from people with shared beliefs.

(Note that this discussion of how the brain works is a very simplified explanation of a very complex system. See the Resources page for books to read if you are interested in learning more)

Tool #3 Story

You hear a lot about stories these days

It is a hot topic in marketing, web sites, video, social media. Everyone needs to be telling stories. Unfortunately, there is a lot of misinformation.

We all think we intuitively know what a story is. And that is true. As humans we are hardwired for story. We are all hardwired to breathe —that doesn't make us experts in the respiratory system

If you look the word story up in a dictionary you will see many definitions from plot, narrative, rumor, news article, lie. These may all be stories but so many definitions create serious dilemmas for marketers learning to use stories.

Most advice centers on topics like how to create a likeable character. How to add drama to the story. Conflict and resolution. Using emotional language. Plot arcs. Hero Journeys.

The problem is this approach is all about how to write a story, and only one type of story at that, not what a story is. You can't get from the process of writing a story back to the definition. It works the other way 'round.

When you understand what a story is you can create a myriad of story types.

Stories are really sharing emotions.

That is because the essence of story is the communication of an emotional event. (Thanks to Annette Simmons for this definition in her book *Whoever Tells the Best Story Wins*)

When you come at it with this definition a whole new world of storytelling and branding opportunities is before you.

Let's look at the three components of that definition: Communication. Emotional. Event.

Communication isn't limited to just words. Melodies communicate. Sounds, like sirens, communicate. Fragrances communicate. Images communicate. And we can (and must) use all of these in our branding efforts.

Stories are all about emotion. Did the guy get the girl? Did the family escape the fire? Did Frasier ever get back with Lilith? We already discussed the need for an emotional component to all our buying decisions and that branding is all about creating the emotional fulfillment that our customers seek. **Any random emotion won't work. It must be emotions that get our customers to stick with us.**

Something has to happen. Often this comes from an event in our past lives. The smell of apple pie brings back memories of your grandmother baking. A song reminds you of your high school boyfriend. The crackling of a fire on a winter evening reminds you of cozy nights in your cabin at Lake Tahoe. Each of these events in your life has an emotional reminder of love, joy, comfort. It could also be fear, worry, shame, but for our branding we are focusing on positive emotions.

When working with stories you can't control the emotion a person will feel. A crackling fire may have negative emotions for someone who watched his house burn down. We can't control every person's reaction to every one of our emotional events. But we can influence the reaction.

If we can't control the emotion of our listener, what do we do? How do we influence the reaction?

The answer is in how we communicate the story.

We can be the teller of a full story. This is what people usually mean when they talk about storytelling. We have a character with an important goal who is struggle against various challenges until she reaches the goal. These are called purpose-told stories because there is a message we are conveying through the story, such as we so believe in forever homes for our animals that we were willing to close the business rather than send any animals to slaughter. Our story shows our commitment to our values. As marketers, we are the authors of these stories

But people are always telling themselves stories as they go through their day. Anything can trigger a story. A mention of your sister's name. A photo of a dog. The aroma of cinnamon. A snub by a colleague.

To think only of the full story we tell our customers (like our founding story) and the totally listener generated story (which might be they are skeptical of the claims we are making) is to miss out on the richness of the spectrum of stories that exist between these two extremes.

Think of it like a sliding scale where the more information we give, the less the listener needs to provide. The opposite is equally possible. We give a few details and let our listener create their own version of the story.

Product descriptions may just set the scene for its use but it is enough for the reader to see herself in the outcome. So this partial story is enough to get our customer to view our product favorably.

Words create stories. Images create stories. Sounds create stories. Each of us will react uniquely to the same word. "Elite" may be enticing to someone with a big ego and looking for a trophy home but a turn-off for someone looking for a friendly neighborhood. Images can create stories. That photo of the Hawaiian beach may be compelling for someone starved for a vacation and living through a Minnesota winter. But it may be cringe-inducing for someone who remembers being dumped by a boy friend on a beach vacation. Sounds create stories. Sounds call up memories from out past. They warn us of danger. They calm our nerves.

So yes, an image can be 10,000 words. But the challenge is: whose words? You don't want the reader to make up any story. You want to make sure it is the story you want them to tell.

How do you do that?

Seed the story. Know their story you want to trigger, use the right medium, provide context, provide direction. Images should have captions or else have text that sets the stage for the story you want. You explain why you are using lavender scent in your brochure. You use related sensory elements so people see the connections and tell themselves the "right" story.

This mix of stories creates the brand and evokes the feeling we have for a company.

Focus on the story the customer is telling herself. This is the most important concept in this book. Everything you do should be with the intention of setting off the story you want her to tell.

☑ Assignment

Think of businesses you love and what sort of stories they tell. Have they set the stage for you to create stories you tell yourself? When you hear their name do you immediately think of some sensory element? Or does the sensory element remind you of them? Or is it that you feel part of their tribe with shared values?

Tool #4 Journey Mindset

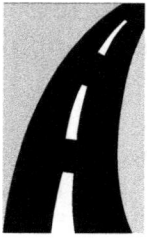

Your Marketing Cycle

Your Customer's Journey

How these two tie together

Your Marketing Cycle

See the diagram on the next page for the Know-Like-Trust-Try-Buy-Repeat-Refer cycle. This is the cycle you are on as you move a customer from awareness of what you do to becoming a Sticky Customer who loves you and brings you not only her repeat business but also friends.

At each step on the cycle you have the ability to influence the behavior of the customer. At each step your customer may say yes or no. You want continued yeses. How can you make this happen? By understanding what is going on at each step. By seeding the story that will get her to say yes and move to the next step.

The you create appropriate marketing for that step. For example, if you have a newsletter, you may want to have one that is for new people who signed up so you can tell them about your product or service and get them comfortable with you. For long time customers, you want to build a sense of tribe. You want them to know their long connection to you brings special rewards. This is the opposite of most cable/phone companies who give the rewards to people as incentive to sign up and then offer little of value to their long-time subscribers. How do you feel when you see those ads offering a great deal to new subscribers? What is the story you tell yourself?

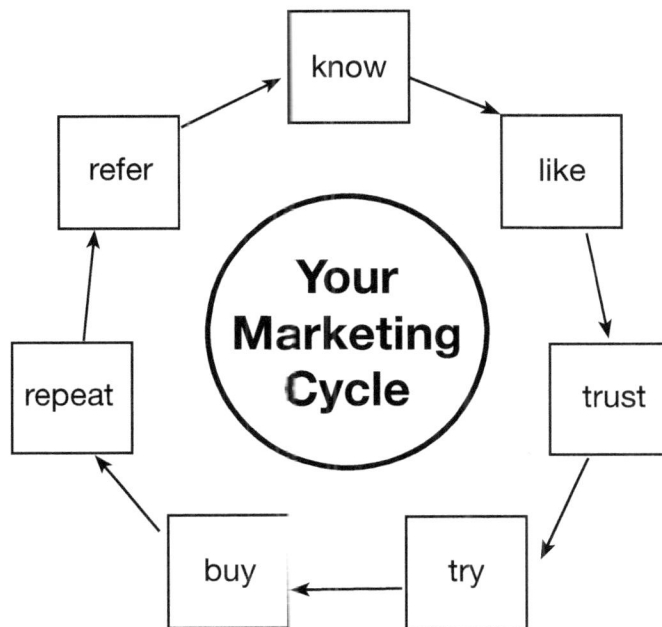

Your Marketing Cycle

know
like
trust
try
buy
repeat
refer

Your Customer's Journey

At the same time your customer is on her own journey. From realizing a need, problem, or desire, to finding possible solutions, evaluating the risk vs. reward of each, weighing options, looking for a low risk way to try the product or service, and finally making a choice.

The customer journey is not just a transaction but the culmination of a journey of many steps. At each of the steps she has a chance to turn from you to another option. The option might be to buy from a competitor, do it herself, spend the money on an alternative solution (she may decide not to take that vacation but create her own staycation instead) or do nothing.

These are all viable options. Your job is to make sure she keeps saying yes at each step.

Success is when Your Marketing Cycle aligns with Your Customer's Journey

Look at the diagram on page 24 and you will see the two journeys have been interwoven. Now as you work through your brand recipe your ideas will not just be random stuff you can do. They can be thoughtfully crafted to match with each step your customer is taking.

Your Customer's Journey

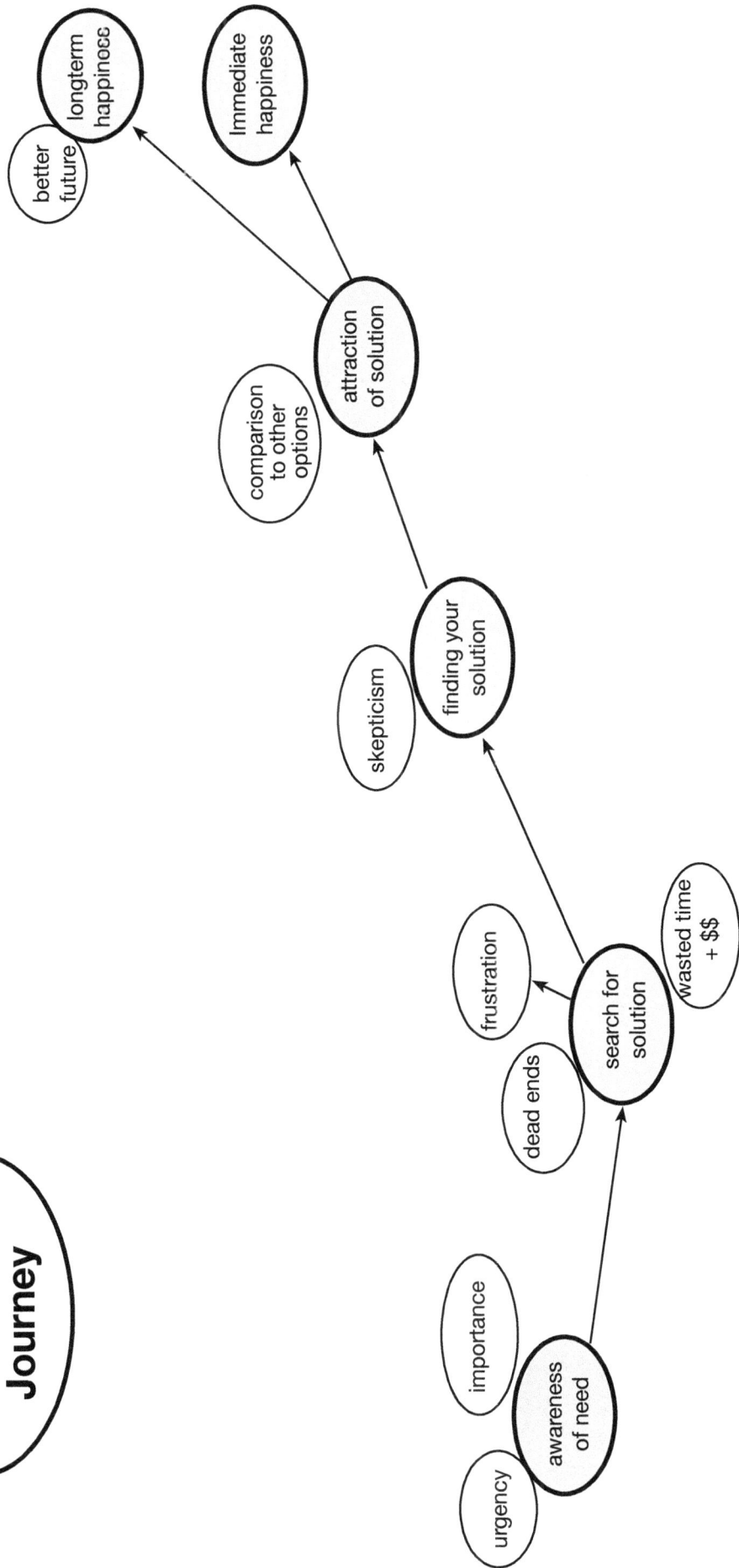

better future

longterm happiness

Immediate happiness

attraction of solution

comparison to other options

finding your solution

skepticism

frustration

search for solution

wasted time + $$

dead ends

importance

awareness of need

urgency

Aligned Journeys

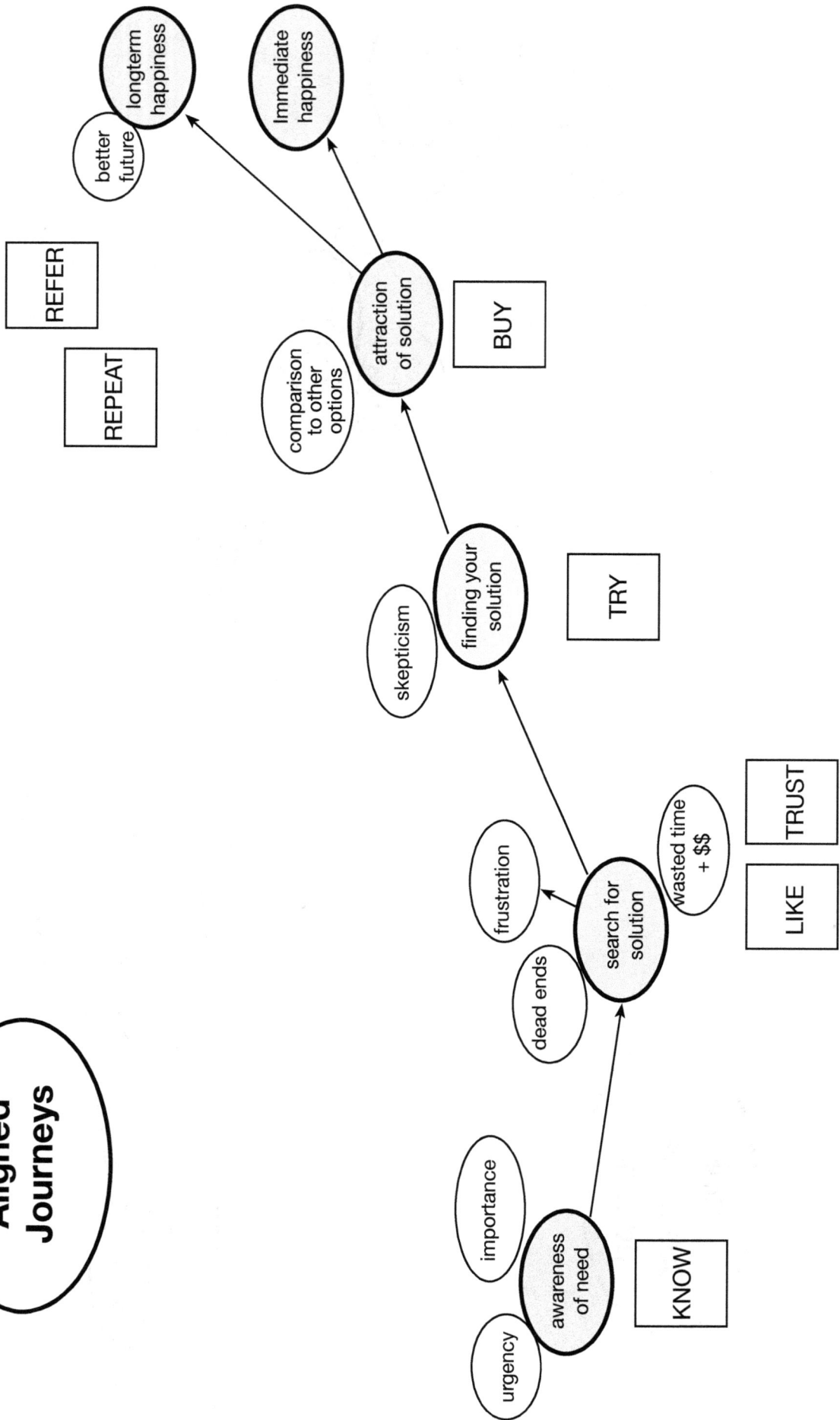

awareness of need — KNOW
- urgency
- importance

search for solution — TRUST / LIKE
- dead ends
- frustration
- wasted time + $$

finding your solution — TRY
- skepticism

attraction of solution — BUY
- comparison to other options

REPEAT

REFER

longterm happiness
- better future

Immediate happiness

Tool #5 Possibilities Mindset

Always be on the lookout for new ideas. Give them a chance to prove themselves, rather than jumping in with "we tried that," "it won't work," "we can't afford that." I sometimes meet clients who are immediately on the defensive to any idea. And sure, my idea may be lousy but it could contain the germ of something wonderful. Sadly, we will never know as it never had the chance to blossom. It was stamped out before it could sprout.

Train yourself to always be watching what others are doing. Not so you can copy them but so that one idea (theirs) can be a springboard to a better idea (yours).

Henry Ford is praised for coming up with the modern assembly line as a way to produce low cost cars. But that idea didn't come out of a vacuum. He had visited other types of companies looking for ideas, including a meat processing plant. As a result he saw the value of moving the work to the worker which cut down assembly time and used less skilled labor over the old method of skilled craftsmen who could do the entire process. What does a meat processor have to do with automobiles? Nothing. But Ford saw that he could reverse the process. They were taking a whole animal and breaking it down to usable parts. He saw he could flip that and take individual parts and make a whole car. Faster and with cheaper labor.

If he had only visited other automobile makers he would never have seen that process.

Always look for the story. If you can discover the story behind the action, you can learn from it. Learning someone else's story gets you out of the reactive, defensive or negative mode it is easy to be in. Why did that driver cut you off or jump ahead to take the last parking spot? You first reaction is negative. Yell at them. Honk the horn. But why might they be doing it? Somebody else just cut them off? Perhaps they are late to a doctor appointment. When you understand someone else's story you are no longer victim to your first negative thoughts.

This immediate reaction is very common and an easy trap to fall into. But with practice you can get out of this trap.

Try small first. So what good does it do to understand the story? Now that you know they are late to the doctor appointment, so what? Maybe nothing will come of it. But it can start you thinking about what made the person late, how can they easily notify the office about their tardiness. Maybe maybe even ideas for reducing the stress of the situation so their blood pressure isn't sky night when they do get to the office. This example probably isn't relative to you unless you are an app developer, a stress reduction coach or perhaps and organizational consultant. But in everyday interactions with your customers you will see many situations that indicate problems, and frustrations in their lives that you might be able to alleviate.

Start taking your new ideas out for a spin. Try a new product (promotion, advertsiement, packaging or whatever) on a few customers. Get input. Accept (encourage!) criticism. Refine. This is the minimum-viable-anything process.

You didn't fail. You just ran an experiment. I have seen a major growth in my own work by saying I will give it a try and use this opportunity as an experiment. I didn't fail; what did I learn? How can I do it better next time. You never have to say "I failed." Instead, you say "I was trying out a new idea."

Actually I usually say that I was auditioning a new idea. I was watching it perform. It isn't me. I don't have to be attached to it. I don't have my ego wound up with it. You may be surprised at how willing you are to try things if you are not so invested in its success.

☑ Assignment

Keep a notebook for your ideas. Write everything down. You may not have a use for it now, but it maybe useful later. Or several thoughts may combine it to a blockbuster idea. Stuck for ideas? Take a nap. When you are going to sleep think about the challenge you are facing. There is a good chance your brain will work on the idea while you sleep and you will have a new idea in the morning.

When looking for a good idea, the advice is to sleep on it.

Your Ingredients

The ingredients of your brand are those ways you touch your customer. They create emotional connections that you nurture. They are all chosen because they appeal to your Vital Few, connect with your beliefs and will give your Vital Few a reason to choose you over other options. These emotional connections are repeated and strengthen the bond.

- **Your beliefs**

- **Your appearance**

- **Your voice**

- **Your sensory elements**

- **Your rituals**

- **Your actions**

Your Beliefs

Business plans always include a section for company values. Sadly, I have found that asking for values gets a useless response.

We are professional. Or competent. Or customer-focused. We have integrity. Or passion.

Wegmans grocery chain uses Caring, High Standards, Making a Difference, Respect, and Empowerment.

Gag. What do any of these mean? How would you see it in action? Can you use this value to help in your business decisions? Would any two people in your company (or customers) agree on exactly what these mean? Probably not. They are too vague, ill-used, abused.

I switched to asking people for their beliefs.

Ah! Now we are getting somewhere. To describe your belief, you have to make a full statement. That usually results in specifics and details.

Here are a few belief statements

Warby Parker (online prescription eyeglasses): We believe that buying glasses should be easy and fun. It should leave you happy and good-looking, with money in your pocket.

Blue April (home delivery of cook-at-home meals) We believe you're never done learning in the kitchen. Our recipes are created to encourage our home chefs to try new ingredients and cooking techniques every week, while honoring our philosophy of seasonal eating. We take great care to ensure that our recipes are suitable for beginner chefs and experts alike.

Kashi (organic grains) Innovative nutrition is our approach to food. It means we value whole food and put the inherent nutrition of food first when considering every ingredient. It means we make our food with a plants-first mindset. It means we value not just the foods we make, but also how we make them by being progressive and mindful of sustainable and ethical farming practices.

Dave's Killer Bread We believe everyone is capable of greatness. We believe in the power of reinvention, and are committed to turning second chances into lasting change.

Subway (fast food sandwiches) We believe that the only way to eat is fresh, made in front of you by real people in a place that you want to visit.

Notice how these belief statements include the customer. They want customers to have good vision, to have fun, eat better, learn to cook, get a second chance.

By opening up their beliefs they attract people who share them.

Are you ever eager to visit a store because they are "professional"? Of course not. Frankly, being professional should be the expected standard. Don't you wonder about businesses that proclaim they are honest? Really? Is this the best they can come up with?

Belief statements help us see the better world this company is helping to build. And we want to be in that world as well.

One other thought: a belief is not a slogan.

Your slogan may come from thinking about your beliefs but don't get caught up in trying to make a catchy tag line. Your beliefs are the serious underpinning of your business. They are not your marketing.

Author C.S. Lewis said, "Integrity is doing the right thing, even when no one is watching."

The same goes for your beliefs. Don't confuse them with marketing.

☑ Assignment

What are your beliefs? Write down your first thoughts. Throughout the day write down new ideas as they come to you. Then review the list and cross out those that don't have room for your customers. Your Vital Few are searching for a company to share their beliefs. Let it be yours.

Your Appearance

How you look is one of the most utilized ingredients of any company's brand. Humans are very visual creatures so this is natural.

But how much thought have you given to your entire appearance?

Did you decide on some colors and a logo and think that is all?

How you look includes your signage, your packaging, your store front, your web site, your business cards, your invoices, your emails, your display racks, your web site's 404 error page. The list goes on.

Everything someone sees that represents you needs to be intentionally created and consistent.

Now you know why I said to find a system to manage your branding ingredients. This list can get very long.

Start with your colors

You need to track your colors. And that means you need to know your color specifications. If it is a color used on the web or digital media then you probably need its RGB (red, green, blue) value or its hex equivalent.

If you have that some color for print then you need the CMYK (cyan, magenta, yellow black) specifications.

You will need these definitions so you might as well start now by identifying them and storing the information where you can easily find it.

Then move on to your logo

Do you need multiple versions? A full color? A black and white? One for use on a colored background? One for a white background? If it is a wide logo do you need a vertical version as well? What about one sized for an avatar? A favicon?

Maybe you don't all of these today but you will eventually. So start organizing them now. Trust me. This will save you a lot of time and frustration.

And then other layouts.

Every time you create a flyer, postcard, coupon or brochure, save a copy.—digitally or make a physical scrapbook.

Having these pieces means you aren't always starting from scratch. Reuse ideas and layouts that worked before. Also, by keeping all of these visual pieces in front of you, there is less risk of veering off course. It means you are developing a good habit which is easy to keep going.

What about all your other visual pieces?

Track down every place you are seen.

All of these visual pieces become your style. And your style should remain consistent so people will recognize you. You can tell an Apple ad from a Harley ad even if there is no logo. They have two completely different styles. Strive to be as distinctive as these brands.

What other visual elements do you have?

Do you have employee uniforms? Or do you wear a signature brooch like former Secretary of State Madeleine Albright? Do you have a signature hair style or color. Well known blogger Henneke always wears a purple blouse. A local cheese-monger sports a huge Mohawk hair cut that is decorated for the season. Sonia Simone of Copyblogger is known as the Pink-Haired Marketer. Maybe you have unique tattoos.

What about your packaging? Apple has raised packaging to an art form and the unwrapping of a new Mac is a ritual in itself.

If you have a storefront, what does it look like? Your shelving and display cases? Your menu?

If you are a consultant, perhaps you have a distinctive briefcase?

Anything visual that identifies you belongs in this category.

One parting thought

Are you one of those people who fusses over your hair, but fails to notice your scuffed shoes? Ever left the house with a button missing? Or get into the sunlight to realize you are wearing black pants and shoes but with navy socks?

I am usually very aware of these details but once I had a major failure while on a business trip. I had carefully packed a business suit and all the related pieces. To make my life easier I had several pairs of the same style of pumps but in different colors. I grabbed a pair and off I went. To may horror, the next morning while getting dressed I realized that I had one navy shoe and one black. Worse, they were both left shoes! There was no way I could put that left shoe on my right foot (trust me, I tried). So that left me with three choices: wear only only one shoe, go barefoot or wear my travel athletic shoes.

I chose the athletic shoes thinking that since I was doing a software demo I would be sitting down and maybe no one would notice.

No such luck. When I arrived I discovered we were using a projection room with stadium seating! I had no desk to hide behind. Everyone in the audience was perfectly positioned to stare at my feet. Because I didn't take care in packing my shoes, I ended up making my shoes a focal point of my presentation. No doubt everyone there forgot most of what I said in the presentation but they all knew about my shoes.

Don't let this happen to you with your branding. Even the smallest details matter.

☑ Assignment

Start gathering your visual brand ingredients. Pull together logo samples, color charts, printouts of your web pages, flyers, brochures, etc. Spread it out in front of you. Does it represent you? Is it all consistent?

Take note of everything you use that is seen by a customer. Is it a generic version because that was the affordable way to get started? Is now the time to upgrade and make these part of your visual branding? Continuing to use generic pieces is a weak spot. Upgrade when your budget allows.

Your Voice

Hi!

What you say covers more than you might think.

First there is the tone of voice

Are you soft and comforting? Or a tough-as-nails drill sergeant barking out orders? One isn't better than the other. They are just different and you need to find the tone of voice that works for your Vital Few.

Do you use a lot of slang? Swear words? That has become more popular as language gets more blunt. Possibly even brutal. But it doesn't work for everyone.

Some need to be inspiring and motivational. Others are supportive and understanding.

Finding your tone of voice can take time. That's OK. Let it evolve. Just realize you need to define your tone so that others can write for your business. You may hire copywriters and they need to speak with your voice. Any staff (and contractors) will need to know the voice of your business to do their jobs well.

What are your sacred words?

Are there words that are used in your industry? Over and out. Roger that. FIFO. Social graph. SEO. Then there are words that are used thanks to text messaging and social apps. brb. rotfl. tmi. TLDR.

Businesses frequently have insider words that their loyal fans know. These words mark the newbie when they must ask what the words mean. Starbucks Venti vs Grande. The In-and-Out Burger 4X4. Or Animal Style. Apple's Genius Bar.

Your tag line falls in the sacred words category.

What other words do you use consistently? Your email signature? How you answer the phone? How you start a workshop or what you say when wrapping a purchase?

Do you have useful metaphors or comparison?

Are you the Uber of lawnmowers or the Nespresso of kale smoothies? Watch what you write and what you say and notice when certain words and phrases are repeatedly used. These may your sacred words. Of course, be sure these are what you want people to remember and not just an old speech habit.

What is your writing style?

Do you write short sentences? Perhaps treating fragments as sentences? Crisp language is your hallmark?

Or maybe you have a more academic style. Long sentences. Clauses. Lots of Oxford commas. Maybe even the dreaded passive voice. If it is right for your audience, fine. Just make sure your audience is up for your more difficult-to-read writing style. If you want to know how you are doing, try using the Hemingway App (http://www.hemingwayapp.com/) and run some of your text through for an analysis.

Your Product Names?

Product names (and service names) are sacred words as well. They should be unique to you and extend your brand personality. We know Apple products by the ever-expanding list of iProducts. Harley Davidson uses words like FatBoy, Street 500, LowRider, Road King. How do your product names stack up? Are they clearly identifiable to you or are they more generic? You aren't using the old standby of Gold, Silver and Bronze membership levels are you?

You have no sacred words? Then now is a good time to see where you might be able to create some. Sacred words are used by people who belong. If you are building a tribe, you need ways to indicate who is in. Those people know the sacred words.

☑ Assignment

Think about your words. Where are there places for sacred words? How can you use words to create a sense of belonging?

Do you have a distinctive tone of voice? Should you have one?

Do your product/service names sound like they belong to you?

Your Signature Sensory Elements

The tricky, and often ignored, brand ingredient: signature sensory elements. Many companies ignore this entirely but when used correctly it can be very powerful

If you are a spa owner, sensory ingredients will be a natural part of your branding. Fragrant candles burning. Steamy herbal teas waiting. The soothing texture of body creams. Warm and snugly robes. Calming pictures on the wall. You have all the bases covered.

But what if you have an IT installation business? Ooh. Not so easy to think of sensory ingredients here!

Even if you are a business consultant, sensory ingredients are so tied up in memories they are worth seeking for your business. You won't be able to use them all (probably) and may not even want to. Perhaps one or two perfect sensory ingredients are all you need. Let them shine on their own rather than being part of a noisy sensory experience.

The sensory ingredients you need to think about

Sounds. Think bells ringing. Jingles. Music. Audible alerts. The sound of a computer booting up. Old fashioned cash registers. Up tempo music in fast food places but slower softer music in for lingering restaurants. Can you take one of your everyday sounds and make it your own? Use it in a surprising way? Check out the HaagenDazs timer to make sure your ice cream is at the right temperature and enjoy the song while you wait. Just point your iPhone at the carton: https://www.youtube.com/watch?v=vYJWifof8vY

Fragrance. We usually think in terms of perfumes or outdoor fragrances. But what about that new car smell? Or the fresh cut wood of a new fence going up? A fragrance will either be obvious or difficult. If you come up empty, let it rest. One will come if it belongs to you.

Taste. This is easy if you have an ice cream shop. You can offer the flavor of the day. Or have a signature flavor. But if you are a financial advisor, what about a bowl of unusual peppermints sitting out for every client meeting?

Texture. Easy if you are a fabric store. Or a furrier. Harder if you are an online business. Perhaps though it can be in your packaging. A jewelry store may use velvet or silk pouches. A local shoe store wraps your shoe boxes in rough twine. (This is a two-fer as it has the texture of the twine plus it is a ritual at the cash register.)

You may think yourself lucky if you have an obvious sensory ingredient to use. But you may want to reconsider. The obvious ingredients are probably used by others in your industry. Does yours stand out? Or do you use gardenia candles and they use rose and you think this is good enough?

It is better to think about ways to make your signature sensory ingredients unique. Surprising. Unexpected.

Once you have one in place, it becomes an agent of anticipation for your customers and will begin to work its magic.

Don't shortchange this thought process. It may take you some time to find your signature ingredients, but it will be worth the effort.

☑ Assignment

Start reflecting on sensory ingredients you might be able to use. Keep a notebook or piece of paper in a handy place so you can jot down ideas as they come to you. Note sensory ingredients that other businesses use. This is not an assignment you can complete in a day. But you can start the quest now.

Your Rituals

We all have daily rituals. Often they are so routine we no longer think about them. We just do them. Brushing our teeth. Making our first cup of tea in the morning. Tying our shoes. The route we take to work or walking the dog can be rituals.

Then there are rituals associated with life's major events. Graduation ceremonies. Weddings. Funerals. Getting the keys to your first home.

In between are the many rituals that enrich our lives. Sending holiday cards. Buying a new car. Buying a prom dress. Our annual closet spring cleaning.

Business need rituals too. Often these just happen. A natural way you greet your customers becomes a ritual through its consistent repetition.

What rituals do you have?

What rituals do you already have in place? Walk through the entire new customer process and see where you have already created rituals. Then do it again with an eye to opportunities for rituals. Walk through the process for repeat customers. And again for unhappy customers. Be especially attuned to the little opportunities for ritual.

Every touch point with a customer is an opportunity. Even opening your newsletter or adding a product to your shopping cart can be rituals. Most of us spend hours on the creation of our newsletters, spell-checking and editing. But do you include yourself on the distribution list and read the newsletter as if you were a customer? Do you intentionally look for places to institute rituals.

Events are rituals

Your yearly employee barbecue? Your customer appreciation event? Your employee of the year announcement? Birthday cards to your customers? A special gift to customers who have been with you for 20 years? Lapel pins awarded to people who have taken 10 tours with your company? To be a ritual these need to be done routinely. They must be dependable or they are not rituals. But they are wonderful for creating that sense of belonging.

Think of several outrageous ideas for rituals. Let your mind wander to the quirky, the unusual, the goofy, the exotic. It must be authentic. It must be appropriate for your Meaningful Few. But most of us play it safe when it comes to new ideas. What can you come up with that is outside the safe zone and make memorable rituals?

A local restaurant uses drink glasses as a container for the bill rather than the usual padded faux leather check presenter. Then the owner decided to make it a bit different by adding stickers with unusual (to the non-restaurant worker) restaurant sayings to the glasses. Each glass had a different saying. It was his way of getting the customer into the chef experience. It became a ritual to read the expression and guess what it meant.

Hidden Rituals

Rituals happen when you are not present with the customer in other ways as well. What happens when they are home with your product? Can unwrapping it be a ritual? Can using it be a ritual? Can connecting with others about it on social media be a ritual? Can recycling the excess packaging be a ritual? Do you include free samples that can be shared with friends?

These invisible (to you) rituals are very powerful and create the nurture factor you need.

☑ Assignment:

Make a list of all the rituals you have in place today. Don't worry if you have none. You can start now with a clean slate! If you have some, reflect on if they are truly the best rituals for your Meaningful Few or can they be improved. Possibly even abandoned. The next step is to think through all the touch points with your clients and brainstorm ideas for rituals. Start with small impactful rituals. Be open to new ones. Let them evolve.

Your Actions

Hmm . . . seems like an odd question for a branding exercise doesn't it? I make products, or I offer services, I go to networking meetings, I handle the billing. You know the "regular stuff."

Well, I am not talking about the regular stuff here.

No, we are talking about what you do to delight your customer and fulfill that inner desire they have.

You have already defined your Vital Few and what will delight them, right? So now I want you to expand on that with the specific, repeatable, intentional things you will be doing to make this happen.

JC Penny made a huge gaffe when it tried to update its pricing. It decided to make things simpler by replacing the confusing array of promotions and coupons with simple everyday low prices. The new policy was implemented by the new CEO Ron Johnson. Johnson had taken this job after working as the Senior VP of Retail Operations at Apple.

Now anyone with half a brain would know that there is little similarity between Apple and JC Penny. Apparently the entire JC Penny Board of Directors combined didn't have half a brain.

Johnson forgot who the customer was. People on fixed budgets. People who have the option of buying similar clothes, shoes, etc. at other stores. People who were loyal to Penny's because of the confusing array of coupons and specials. They loved it. Thrill of the hunt and scoring a bargain.

Johnson thought he was making the system better for his customers. Instead he was taking away their reason for buying.

And those customers left in droves. Revenues dropped 51%. And Ron Johnson lost his job.

So what does this example have as a lesson for you?

Start with what your customers want. Be sure to talk to them. Never be so arrogant that you believe you already know what your customers want. Always be testing your ideas on real customers.

But, "doing" is more than coupons and promotions. Doing can be how you treat people (here it overlaps with what you say and with rituals). It can be contests. It can be special services you offer, like delivery or special orders or custom services.

It can be the fact that you offer packages of services with specific benefits rather than sell your service by the hour.

Or that you have a customer loyalty program. Offer referral bonuses or bring-a-friend promotions.

Maybe you partner with another local business. Or perhaps it is your social consciousness. You support a local non-profit. You follow the Tom's one-for-one model.

You use your beliefs, be it frugal shopping or saving the planet, to inform what you offer and how you offer it.

Understanding your "do" is never done. The ideas you record today are just the start of a long journey to creating a delightful customer experience.

☑ Assignment

Start your "do" list. Don't forget to plan for new ideas so be sure to use a big piece of paper. A sticky note won't work here!

Your Process

Now that you have the mental tools and your initial ingredients identified you are ready to start mixing that glue.

You can't make a souffle by just dumping the eggs, butter, sugar in a pan and sticking it in the oven. There is a careful process of creating air in the mixture through beating the egg white, carefully folding in the other ingredients without losing the volume and baking at the right temperature without opening the door. Even after it comes out, you need to make sure it is not disturbed until it has cooled and the structure has set. Don't follow these rules and you end up with a goupy mess or a flat souffle.

And so it is with your ingredients.

I often get push back from clients about when I ask about some of their brand ingredients. They are quick to tell me that they are using good images, but then ignore the fact that they don't use captions or provide other context so the reader gets the desired story.

Intentional. Consistent. These are the two words you must always think about and follow.

Intentionally select your brand elements. Understand the story your customer is telling herself, the story you want Customer Journey diagram and plot where you can use specific branding elements to strengthen your emotional connection with your customer at that point. Your goals is to have these glue points at each step. Some will have more branding opportunities than others. That is OK. But you want to have something at each point.

Consistently use it. You can't forget to wear your store uniform. You can't be hit-and-miss with your greetings. You can be serious and academic one day and telling jokes the next. Lack of consistency confuses and annoys people. They want a consistent experience or will go somewhere else.

Develop checklists and processes so that everyone on your staff knows how your brand acts and delivers the experience your customer is expecting.

Story Is the Liquid in Your Recipe

Ever have one of those light bulb moments? You are working on a problem and out of the blue comes something totally unrelated and yet a perfect solution to what you are working on?

Well that happened to me as I was reading the book *Ingredient: Unveiling the Essential Elements of Food* by Ail Bouzari. It is an entertaining read about the basics of food: water, sugars, carbohydrates, etc. and what is going on at the molecular level when you cook. Bouzari states that **"Water is important: it's the theater in which the other ingredients perform."**

That comment was a light bulb moment for me.

Story is the water in your brand recipe

Let's explore this a bit.

If you think about food you make, how many recipes have no liquid (water)? Mixed nuts? That is about all. Even rubs for meat and fish only work once the juices interact with the spices to release their flavor.

Most recipes use water to combine the individual ingredients as water changes the way the other ingredients interact. Even foods, say an apple, that look solid are really masses of cells with trapped juices. Our job is usually to chop, mash, puree, and/or heat those foods to get that juice released. It is only once those juices are flowing that what you are cooking morphs from discrete ingredients into the dish you want to eat.

Liquid water is only one of its forms. We use the power of gaseous water (steam) to get bread, cakes and soufflés to rise.

And without frozen water we would have no gelato. And the world would be a much the poorer place without it.

That is the perfect analogy for story.

If you look at story as the theater in which your brand ingredients perform you have a better sense of how integral story is to your marketing/branding.

Story is no longer something you add on like a ribbon on a package. Story is not an isolated customer success or even your telling of the founding of the business.

Instead story is the theater in which all your brand ingredients interact to create the feeling you want customers to have about you. They work together to fulfill your customer's inner desire.

This may be a new concept and you may be asking, what exactly does this mean? How do I do this? I don't even know where to start?

Well, I am glad you asked.

Let's look at an example

Remember just as water can be a liquid, a solid (ice) or a gas (steam), stories can be purpose-told or user-created or anything in between. You use these various incarnations depending on your situation and goal.

When you have an important message you want to communicate, you use a purpose-told story with all its details, conflict, hero, etc.

Other times you want the customer to create their own story.

Take a signature fragrance you may want to use.

What is your story about using it this fragrance? Why use any fragrance? Why this fragrance over another one? What is the emotion you are trying to convey? How does this fit in your overall brand plan to satisfy your customer's inner goal?

Now ask yourself:

What is the story my customer is telling herself when she walks into my spa? That I am a sanctuary in her hectic life? That visiting my store is energizing? That I remind her of her youth?

Then:

Is this the story you want her to tell? Does this fragrance support it? How does it work with the other ingredients you have in place? Are they all part of the same story? Or at least aligned rather than in conflict.

A fragrance usually is a completely customer-created story. You seed the story with the fragrance and the customer takes it from there based on her own experience and biases.

Is this what you want? Or do you need to provide more context? What is the risk of her creating her own story?

You can seed the emotional reaction by explaining how lavender is soothing. It can treat headaches and exhaustion and promote easier breathing. It has wonderful nostalgic properties.

You let your customers know you have purposefully selected lavender as your signature fragrance. You create the expectation for lavender at every visit. You never use gardenia just to switch things up.

The goal is that lavender becomes a positive association with your business.

But it only works consistently if you have set the stage: You intentionally choose the fragrance. You use it consistently. You mention why this fragrance is your choice–which can be a casual remark or a major point in your promotional materials. You get to choose.

You are intentionally forging the relationship between the fragrance and the customer's experience with your business.

What you are really doing is getting the customer to tell herself the story of how good she feels by visiting your spa. In some cases the customer may not consciously understand what is going on. But she knows how your business makes her feel.

This emotional story brings the magic to your brand ingredients.

A fragrance by itself may have little to no impact on a customer. But a story a customer tells herself about that fragrance is an essential ingredient in your brand recipe. If you use the same fragrance consistently it becomes a trigger for your story in the customer's mind.

When looking at the ingredients you want to use, consider each ingredient is part of the whole experience. You probably wouldn't put chopped onions in your chocolate layer cake. Don't add any brand ingredients that don't enhance your other ingredients. Don't add ingredients that aren't the starting point for a story.

And always be thinking about its sticky value. Don't add ingredients just because you can. Add them because they up the sticky value of the overall brand experience.

☑ Assignment

Thinking of story as the water in your brand recipe is probably a new idea. So today why not just noodle on this idea today. Be alert to brand ingredients as you go about your day. Focus on your business and/or others you interact with. Be conscious of the story you are telling yourself when you experience a story ingredient.

Story As Proof

Story is communication. Story can be entertainment. Story persuades. Story is fundamental to being a human being.

But story is also proof.

Marketers routinely write claims about their products and services. We are 42% faster than the competition. Our widget is 10 times stronger than the other brand. These are claims that can be verified.

Do you remember the section on Beliefs? How they form the foundation of your brand and connect with your Vital Few?

So often we come up with aspirational beliefs. We want to be the best. We want to be customer-centric. But we often fall short because these pronouncements are not underpinned with reality.

The way to prove your chosen belief statements are true is to identify a story (or at least an anecdote) that proves it.

John Jantsch is the creator or Duct Tape marketing and has written a very insightful article on the Four Stories Every Business Must Build.

Here is one of them that provides the background to his positioning as a practical marketing consultant.

Early on in my marketing consulting business I was invited to be part of a pitch for a very large piece of business. It was a national firm that wanted to hire a national ad agency, but also include a local marketing support company for the local branch.

The New York ad agency sent five people, all clad in black head to toe and armed with a 100-page deck filled with research and recommendations.

When it came time for me to offer my two cents I said something like – I don't know, why don't we just talk to some of your current customers? The meeting ended and the next day the VP that was conducting the search called and said he wanted me to do the entire project without the New York ad agency. To this day I can hear him say why – "you were the only one that said anything that was practical."

Ah, as practical as anything named Duct Tape should be!

If you have a stated belief but no proof story to back it up, you need to rethink the belief. If you make claims about your product but have no customer proof story, then maybe you need to hold off on promoting that claim until you do.

Story is the perfect tool to put your ideas to the test. Use stories to ground your business in reality and keep you from veering off into the weeds of marketing hype.

☑ Assignment

Go back and look at your beliefs statements you did at the beginning of this process. Do you have stories for each one? If not, start looking for some or put that belief on hold.

Mapping Your Customer Buying Cycle

We talked about checklists before and now is the time to really explore this.

Go back to your buying cycle map. For each step in the know-like-trust-try-buy-repeat-refer cycle identify where and how your brand ingredients will be applied.

You can do this on one big sheet of paper, separate sheets, a Trello board, a scrapbook or a Mind Map. You could even use poster board with sticky notes on it so you have flexibility as you design your customer journey.

It doesn't really make any difference what method you use. But there are a few requirements:

- ♦ You actually have a method
- ♦ You use this method
- ♦ It is always visible (no putting it in a drawer and forgetting it!)

The point is to stay on course

You can get as creative as you like. Add images—either prints or drawings. Samples of biz cards and logo. Feel free to use a specific color for each ingredient category.

Be clear about the stories that are being told and the emotions you are trying to trigger.

When you are done, stand back and look at the whole cycle. How does it look? Robust and engaging? A few holes leading to people dropping out?

Does it look authentic? That you really care? This is important because sometimes we can appear to salesy and turn off people.

Do your beliefs shine through? Shared beliefs are the foundation of a strong brand and too often they are sequestered in the About page where they have minimal impact. Reread your marketing materials and web site. How clear are your values?

Now develop your own checklist for anything that touches a customer.

Each time you write a blog post, send out a newsletter, or design a flyer, you need a checklist to make sure you are staying on message and on brand. If you have volunteers, contract help or new staff they need to know this process so they are following the brand guidelines.

In keeping with the Minimum Viable Brand mindset start small. Don't create something too unwieldy to use. Then add and modify as you go. Learn from your successes and your failures.

When others are doing work for you make sure they give you any specifications you will need in the future. This is especially important with any graphics/web help. What are the specs of the colors they used? Image dimensions? Software used? Locations of the source files? Samples of the finished product?

Knowing all of this will make it so much easier for the next person to carry on efficiently and with consistent results.

Assignment

Start planning your Buying Cycle Checklist. What method will you use? Can you start putting a few pieces on the journey map and then add to it as you go along? All the work you have done so far will only be useful if it gets incorporated into your daily processes. You are so close to the finish line, don't falter now!

Download the Buying Cycle Mind Map or create your own version and start filling it in.

The Power of Surprises

We have been talking about creating stickiness by creating emotional stories through intention and consistency. Talking about surprises may sound like a contradiction

A surprise means you are doing something different. Something that is not expected.

But surprises have tremendous power and have a place in your glue recipe.

A recent study done at Emory University demonstrated that the brain's pleasure center responds more strongly to a pleasurable sensation when it is unexpected. This is the same region of the brain that is activated by cocaine or other drugs. The study may help deal with addiction. But it helps us marketers understand the power of surprise in our marketing efforts.

Remember the day you brought the new car home? You made sure it was polished to a high shine. Maybe you just sat in it for new car smell. You refused to take it to the grocery for fear of a collision with a shopping cart. But over time, the new car smell was replaced with pizza fragrance from your take out dinner. The fender carried a ding from your son's driving lesson. You didn't have time to wash it after the camping trip.

It didn't take that long for it to lose the new and exciting feeling. It became transportation.

We all have experienced the fall off in emotion through repeated exposure. Your husband may have been your teen age heart throb. Every time you saw him you felt that zing. Now you have been married for decades and that zing has long been replaced by other emotions: love, friendship, care.

The loss of the zing isn't a bad thing because it has been replaced by deeper emotional connections.

But we still long for that zing. What can you do?

With surprises! It doesn't have to be a big surprise, like front row tickets to *Hamilton*. Maybe just a small bunch of flowers. Or a bag of M&Ms.

Something that says "I was thinking of you" Something that shows you don't take the relationship for granted. Something to bring a smile to her face.

The same happens with our relationship with companies we support. We were excited to find that shoe store, auto parts supplier or cleaning service that made our heart sing. Over time the song became background music. Not that the service declined or we cared less. It was just that it became routine.

We don't want the relationship with our customers to become mundane. Surprises can work exceedingly well for a business as for a personal relationship.

And yes, we need to intentionally plan for these surprises. If we don't think about adding a dash of surprise, we will forget in the busyness of our lives.

Need a few examples?

In its early days, Amazon would include little gifts like Post-It notes or refrigerator magnets.

Today, Zappos has started decorating the inside of some of their shipping boxes so you can unfold the box and find all sorts of creative ways to use it. (check out: Imnotabox.com)

The Goulet Pen Company is an online/mail order company for fountain pen enthusiasts. I bought a bottle of in from them and it arrived with several personal notes from people in shipping and billing, a book mark and a miniature Tootsie Pop. Why a Tootsie Pop? Well, I called customer support and I found out that the owners have a soft spot for sweets and wanted to share that with their customers.

My local car dealer who placed a red rose on the passenger seat when I picked up my car from service.

Some of these may have been random. Some may become rituals. But all started as a little surprise.

☑ Assignment

What can you do? This is a perfect opportunity to try out different low cost ideas. If one really resonates with your customers perhaps it could become a ritual. Keep a list of your ideas. A few may become rituals, some can be rotated at random intervals to keep them fresh and others may be a one-time thing. Always be looking for new ideas. Like hiding Easter eggs, the joy of finding an egg is matched by the joy of watching someone else's surprised reaction. Enjoy!

For reference, here is the article about the cocaine study: http://www.ccnl.emory.edu/Publicity/MSNBC.HTM

How Strong is Your Brand Glue Recipe?

Is it supporting your Marketing Cycle?

Every customer is on a journey with your brand from initial awareness to becoming a forever fan with repeat purchases and spreading your fame. Your goal is to get them through the buying cycle and into the repeat and refer stages through specific marketing efforts at each stage. If we lose them at any stage, they are problably gone forever.

Awareness

They start at the Awareness phase. Here they learn of your existence. Maybe their friends are talking about you. Or they see an ad. See your booth at the farmer's market. Somehow they get a favorable enough impression that they pay attention.

Like and Trust

The next two steps are crucial. They are the Like and Trust stages.

These are two separate steps. And both are necessary. We don't buy from people we don't like. And we don't buy from people we don't trust.

We all know this but often don't think about how intentionally we will cultivate this like and trust. We think our personality will carry the day. Plus a few testimonials.

If you become a loyal customer at some point you are resistant to leaving them for another option because you have built a bond with them. You like them. How could you abandon them?

We also stick with someone we trust. That doesn't mean we never try a new restaurant. It means we give preference to someone we already have a relationship with and trust that they have our best interests at heart. Once again this is an inner goal at work. We will give up fancier location, newer features or convenience when this business we know has our trust and fulfills our inner goals

Try

The next step is to get this person to Try. Free samples. Free consultation. Low risk/low price introductory course. You see this everywhere, from grocery stores to IT consulting. You want to give the person a taste of your great product/service. Two things happen. One is the more obvious. If someone tries what we offer and they are pleased, they are more likely to buy (or buy again). This sample gives us a chance to make a good impression.

The second aspect of the Try phase is the psychological principle of reciprocity. If we get something from someone we feel the need to reciprocate. Get a taste of that new sausage at the grocery and we feel the urge to buy a package in return. This can be very subtle. So subtle you may not be aware of it happening. But those free samples drive a lot of sales!

Buy

If you get them to try, then you hope to move them along to the Buy step. We do this with easy payment plans, taking credit cards, delivery service, extended hours. Anything to remove potential obstacles and make it easy to buy.

Repeat

Once they buy the obvious next step is to turn them into a Repeat buyer. Most business owners know this intuitively. It is easier to sell to an existing client than find a new one. We do this in the store by remembering their tastes so we can suggest something else they might like. We send birthday cards. Develop loyalty programs. Buy 10-and-get-12 programs.

Refer

The last step is to Refer. How do we get these people to tell their friends? We encourage them to bring-a-friend events. Send a gift after their referred person signs up. And ask them to post positive reviews.

And the cycle begins again with these new customers.

Every stage of this journey are brand story opportunities. Sticky brands use stories at every point to keep customers glued to them.

That doesn't mean that each step has equal weight and equal focus. Each company will have a unique approach.

But if you are not getting enough customers, you need to focus on the Awareness step first. If you get customers but they tend to drift away, then the Repeat step needs serious reflection.

This is the journey you want your customer to complete. What are you doing at each step to propel them along?

✅ Assignment

Stories are the engine of this movement. What stories are you using at each step on your customer's journey? Now would be a good time to start identifying your 7 journey steps and what you do at each one.

Print the Buying Cycle diagram to use with this exercise.

Creating A Minimum Viable Brand

By now you are probably overloaded with great ideas to implement. But just like gorging on M&M's, it can be too much of a good thing.

So what to do? You are thrilled with the possibilities you have come up with. You don't want to lose the momentum. You see that you really can delight your Vital Few.

So now you need to scale back and think in terms of the Minimum Viable Brand.

A Minimum Viable Brand starts when you have the minimum elements in place to attract and retain customers. But the glue is weak. It may be enough for some customers but others will wander off. That's OK. This as a starting point.

The first step to a Minimum Viable Brand is to make sure whatever you are doing now supports the brand feeling you want. So review your logo, web site, flyers, voice messages, emails, etc. Identify your existing brand ingredients and plot them out on your branding Mind Maps.

A Minimal Viable Brand works even on a very small scale, if the synergy of the parts creates a robust whole. Some of the ingredients may not be represented. That's fine as you can add them later. You are creating the foundation so it is critical that your branding efforts are intentional and consistent.

Remember: "Start where you are. Use what you have. Do what you can."

Don't be discouraged if your Mind Maps seem sparse. A Minimum Viable Brand is created when you have the essential pieces in place to create the feeling you want your customer to experience. It may only be a small flame right now but it will become an intentionally nurtured blaze.

Look for places to add ingredients that don't cost money or take too much time. For example, you can create a ritual for greeting your customers. You can make sure your email signature creates the right story.

☑ Assignment

Reflect on what you have in place and what pieces are working well. Look for holes, places to beef up that feeling you are trying to generate. Be as creative as you can. Get ideas from other businesses. Your brain is a marvelous idea generating machine. But sometimes we try to hard. Take a nap and see if when you wake up you don't have some new ideas!

The Evolution of Your Brand Recipe

Think of the versatile carrot cake. If you are a beginning baker, carrot cake is a great place to start. Easy recipe, pretty much guaranteed tasty results. All you need is the basic recipe and a muffin tin. Bake the batter in the tins, pop those little guys out and enjoy. Nothing better for a morning treat.

As your skills improve you can get more elaborate. Bake the batter in square pan and when done sprinkle with confectioner's sugar. Cut into square and you have a lovely luncheon dessert. Then move on to a simple lemon icing for a more professional look, contrasting texture and of course, the lovely lemon tartness to contrast with the sweet cake.

As you get more adventurous you can experiment with layer cakes, adding nuts and fruit bits to the basic cake recipe, try unconventional frosting flavors and finish off with elaborate decorations.

Carrot cake is so versatile. It allows you to start where you are. Add what you have on hand when the inspiration for cake strikes. And be as creative as you want.

So is a brand recipe.

Look at your brand recipe in three stages:

- Brand elements you have now.
- Brand elements you can see are needed and doable
- Great ideas that need more time or money or resources than you have in the near future.

Now let's look at each one

What you have now

Maybe a logo. A tag line. A web site design. Most businesses, no matter how small, start with a few visual branding elements. They don't have to be perfect. They have to be good enough to support your desired brand. And work with what you are using for your minimum viable brand.

This is where you start. Weed out anything that doesn't work for your desired brand feeling. This is the foundation of your brand platform, even if it is just a logo. Better to have a few things that really work together than include anything that is dissonant.

Your obvious next steps

What ideas do you have with that are feasible in the near future? Identifying sacred words and using them more intentionally is an easy place to start. Updating your email signature. Personal greetings. Adding your company beliefs to your web site.

These branding ideas are free so include them. Spend time reviewing the ideas you have been writing down to find those with the most promise. Simple things like how you greet a customer, how you answer the phone, how you sign your emails can be done immediately.

With a small budget you can create thank you cards to include with purchases—and they might even have your brand scent! Consider new printed materials. Update your packaging.

Add to this list as doable ideas come to you. Keep a prioritized list and work the list.

Your big ideas

We all have these great big audacious ideas. Ideas are pretty cheap when you think about it. We throw away more ideas each day than we can possibly remember.

Most of these ideas are not workable. They sound great until you start digging and then they don't hold up. But often in that idea is a germ of something really useful. So write down these ideas in your Dream File.

Let these ideas percolate and transmogrify (for you Calvin and Hobbes fans). You may start to notice patterns. Or possibilities.

Experiment. Try new ideas. Combine several ideas into one. Toss out those that aren't working. Nurture possibilities. Be observant. Keep good records (even if only using a stack of sticky notes) of what is working and why you think other ideas failed. Don't give up.

The most important ingredient to this process is to keep an open mind. Always be alert. Your best ideas will not come from competitors. Those ideas will just be me-too ideas. Instead look at unrelated businesses. Take a walk in the park. Listen to podcasts that have nothing to do with what you do. Take a vacation. Henry Ford came up with the idea for his first-ever auto assembly line after a visit meat packing plant.

This creative ability to take unrelated ideas and come up with something new may take time to develop. It is a muscle you need to train. There are no gym fees with this training. There is no getting up early. There is no sweat involved. Once you go down this road you will find ideas everywhere. And some will be perfect for your sticky brand.

☑ **Assignment**

> Gather up all the ideas you generated during the Branding Sparks drivers exercises. Organize them into the 3 categories: Do Now, Next Steps and Big Ideas. Start to get a feel for your brand experience.

Keeping It Going

Congratulations! You have made it through all the components of a brand. You have a ton of ideas. You can see how you can start small and grow your brand recipe. But don't rest now!

All your great ideas and good intentions will crumble if you don't have a plan to keep your branding efforts going.

Like nurturing any new habit, you need a plan to make it happen. Did you ever plan to go to the gym each morning and it just happened? Probably not. It you did you were a rare person.

Habits don't happen because we have will power. Or good intentions. Or see the benefit. No. A habit happens when we create a system that supports our doing it.

If you plan to go to the gym each morning, make sure your gym clothes are laid out, right beside the bed. When you get up, you will stumble over them. You don't have to think about finding your gym clothes. It is a no-brainer to put them on. And the habit begins to form.

There are many great books on habit-building. If you need a little help try one of these books:

- *The Power of Habit: Why We Do What We Do in Life and Business* by Charles Duhig
- *Succeed: How We Can Reach Our Goals* by Heidi Grant Halvorson
- *Switch: How to Change Things When Change Is Hard* by Chip Heath and Dan Heath

Here are some ideas to think about implementing your branding ideas:

Keep your brand drivers visible

If you have been recording your ideas on paper, hang the pages where you can see them. Sticky notes. Butcher paper on the wall. A clothes line with your thoughts hanging from clothes pins. The more it is in your face, inconvenient and always there, the more likely you will pay attention.

Focus in your Minimum Viable Brand

Be sure you have identified the three tiers of your Minimum Viable Brand. Know what you are doing now and what you want to add as you can. Keep everything consistent. Expand when you can but don't take on so much you can't keep it all going.

Create a checklist

Pilots use checklists of the aircraft and the personnel readiness before they take off. Health care professionals use checklists to make sure the steps to a procedure are completed and in the right order for a successful outcome. Proofreaders use checklists to review the written document before publication. A checklist allows the proofreader to review the document many times, once for each issue. Spelling, punctuation, company style, formatting, etc. Checklists make sure you do a job consistently and correctly every time.

A brand checklist is a useful tool for you to use so your brand does veer off course. Create your own checklist. Get in your Vital Few mindset. Review for your sacred words. Review for your tone of voice / writing style. Have you included sensory descriptors? Does it link to your beliefs? Every time you write a blog post, create a flyer, add a new page to your web site, come up with a promotion, or post on Facebook, use your checklist. You can't add all brand drivers in everything. It isn't possible and it would get annoying. But a checklist will keep you on track and consistent.

Develop a system for new ideas

When new ideas strike, will you be prepared to remember them? It makes no difference if you carry a notebook, use the dictation app on your phone or write them on the palm of your hand. Just record the ideas so you don't lose them. Talk to your best customers and get ideas from them. Talk to your staff. Talk to your vendors. Be open to new ideas coming from unusual places. Great ideas come when you are out for a run, taking a shower or on vacation. Be ready to record them so they don't drift away.

☑ Assignment

It would be a shame to waste the effort you have put into defining your brand ingredients. Think about what is doable. Don't tackle ideas that are out of your reach right now. Just keep chipping away at what you can accomplish. But come up with a plan to keep this going and growing.

Disneyland
Branding Example
Mind Maps

The following pages use Disneyland as a model for the branding exercises. This is not a complete analysis of the brand but a way to give you ideas of how to think about your branding for each of the ingredients.

I chose Disneyland because it is well known and well-respected but also because it has such a wealth of branding glue. It is one of the stickiest brands around and it sticks throughout a person's lifetime.

Disneyland isn't perfect (as those people who go online to note that a lightbulb is out on a sign or that there was a gum wrapper on Main Street or the staff wasn't pleasant). Nobody is perfect. But they come darn close.

Notes and Ideas

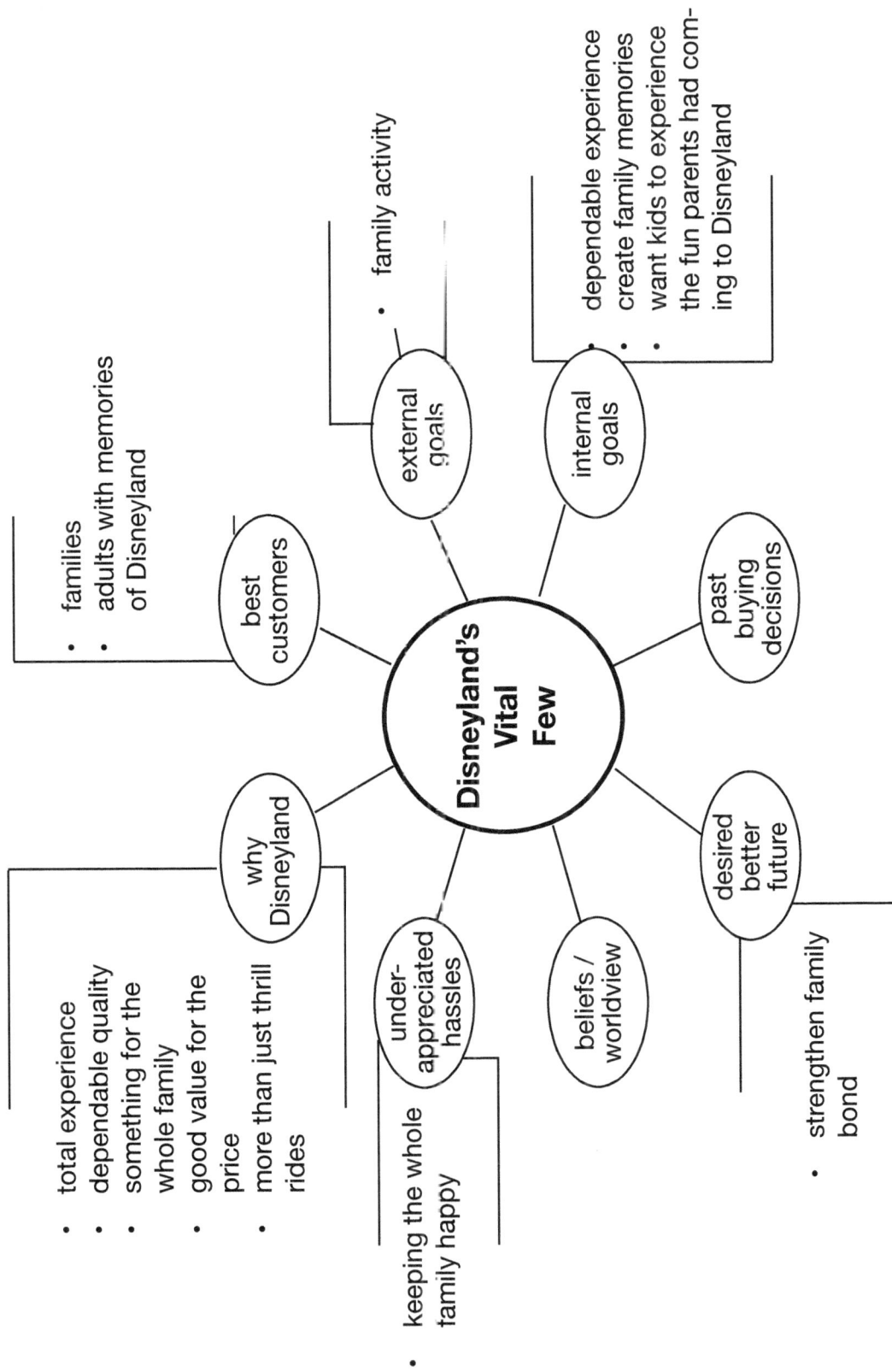

Disneyland's Vital Few

best customers
- families
- adults with memories of Disneyland

external goals
- family activity

internal goals
- dependable experience
- create family memories
- want kids to experience the fun parents had coming to Disneyland

past buying decisions

why Disneyland
- total experience
- dependable quality
- something for the whole family
- good value for the price
- more than just thrill rides

under-appreciated hassles
- keeping the whole family happy

beliefs / worldview

desired better future
- strengthen family bond

Notes and Ideas

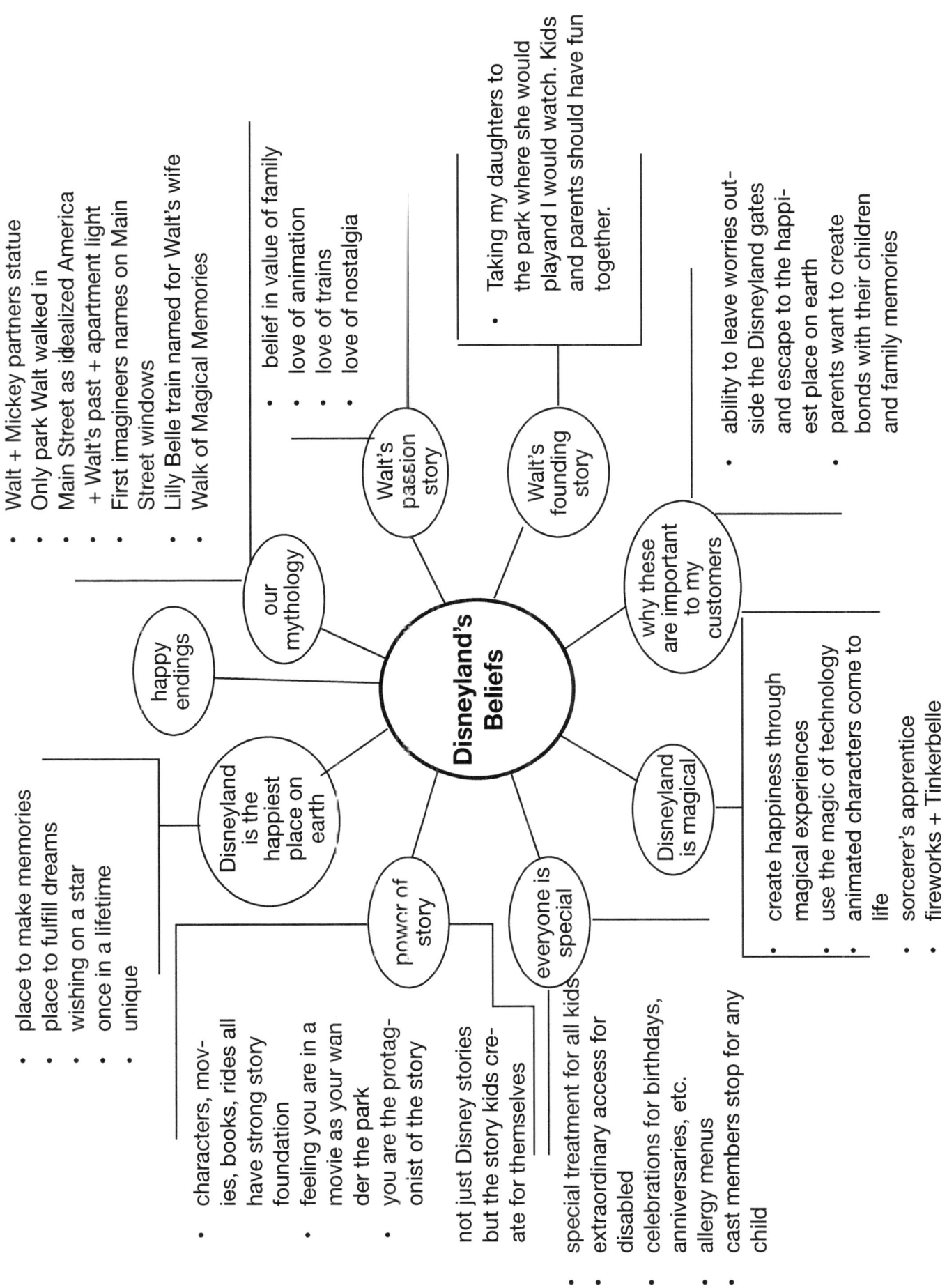

Disneyland's Beliefs

our mythology
- Walt + Mickey partners statue
- Only park Walt walked in
- Main Street as idealized America + Walt's past + apartment light
- First imagineers names on Main Street windows
- Lilly Belle train named for Walt's wife
- Walk of Magical Memories

Walt's passion story
- belief in value of family
- love of animation
- love of trains
- love of nostalgia

Walt's founding story
- Taking my daughters to the park where she would playand I would watch. Kids and parents should have fun together.

why these are important to my customers
- ability to leave worries outside the Disneyland gates and escape to the happiest place on earth
- parents want to create bonds with their children and family memories

Disneyland is magical
- create happiness through magical experiences
- use the magic of technology animated characters come to life
- sorcerer's apprentice
- fireworks + Tinkerbelle

everyone is special
- special treatment for all kids
- extraordinary access for disabled
- celebrations for birthdays, anniversaries, etc.
- allergy menus
- cast members stop for any child

power of story
- characters, movies, books, rides all have strong story foundation
- feeling you are in a movie as your wander the park
- you are the protagonist of the story
- not just Disney stories but the story kids create for themselves

Disneyland is the happiest place on earth
- place to make memories
- place to fulfill dreams
- wishing on a star
- once in a lifetime
- unique

happy endings

Notes and Ideas

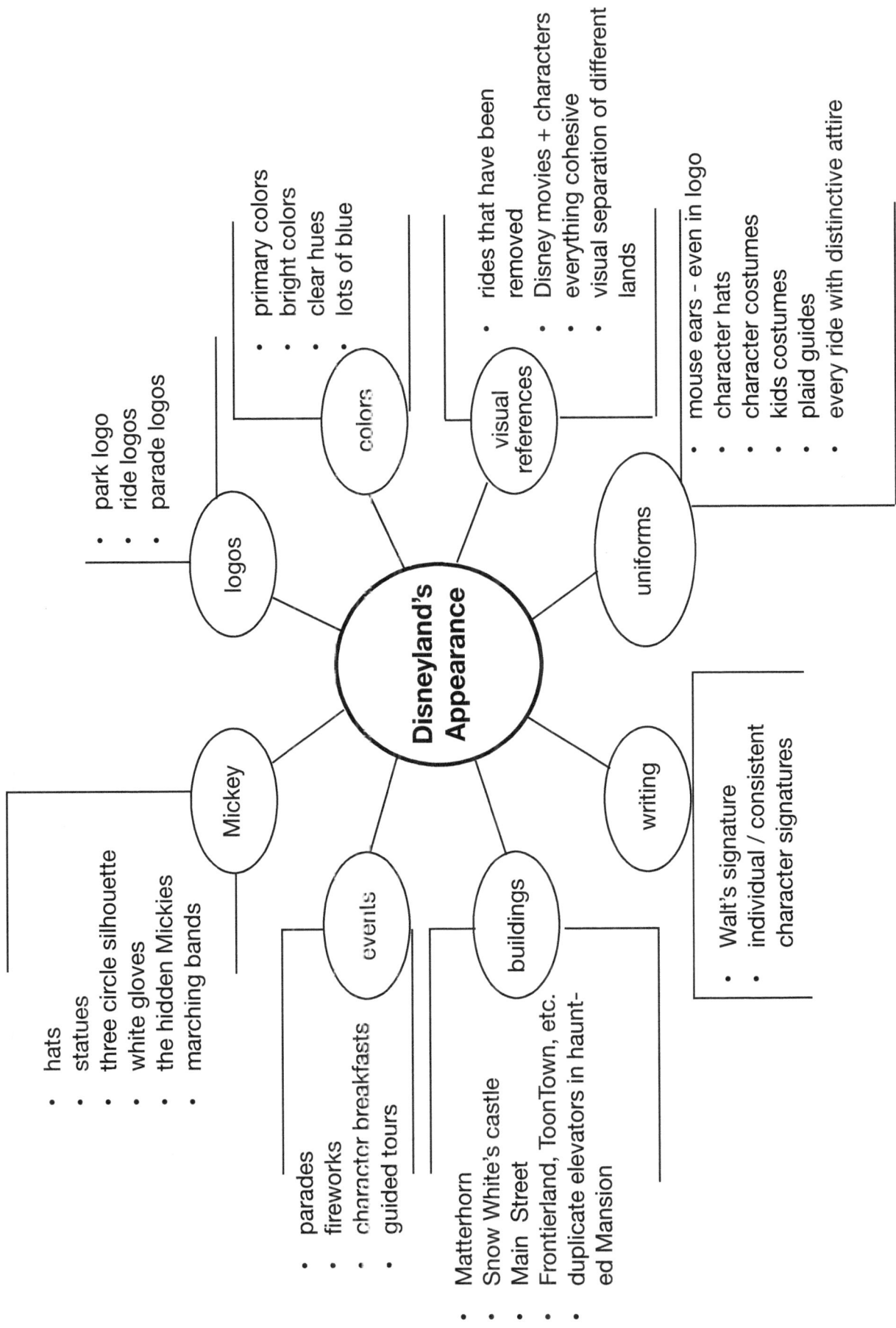

Disneyland's Appearance

logos
- park logo
- ride logos
- parade logos

colors
- primary colors
- bright colors
- clear hues
- lots of blue

visual references
- rides that have been removed
- Disney movies + characters
- everything cohesive
- visual separation of different lands

uniforms
- mouse ears – even in logo
- character hats
- character costumes
- kids costumes
- plaid guides
- every ride with distinctive attire

Mickey
- hats
- statues
- three circle silhouette
- white gloves
- the hidden Mickies
- marching bands

events
- parades
- fireworks
- character breakfasts
- guided tours

buildings
- Matterhorn
- Snow White's castle
- Main Street
- Frontierland, ToonTown, etc.
- duplicate elevators in haunted Mansion

writing
- Walt's signature
- individual / consistent character signatures

Notes and Ideas

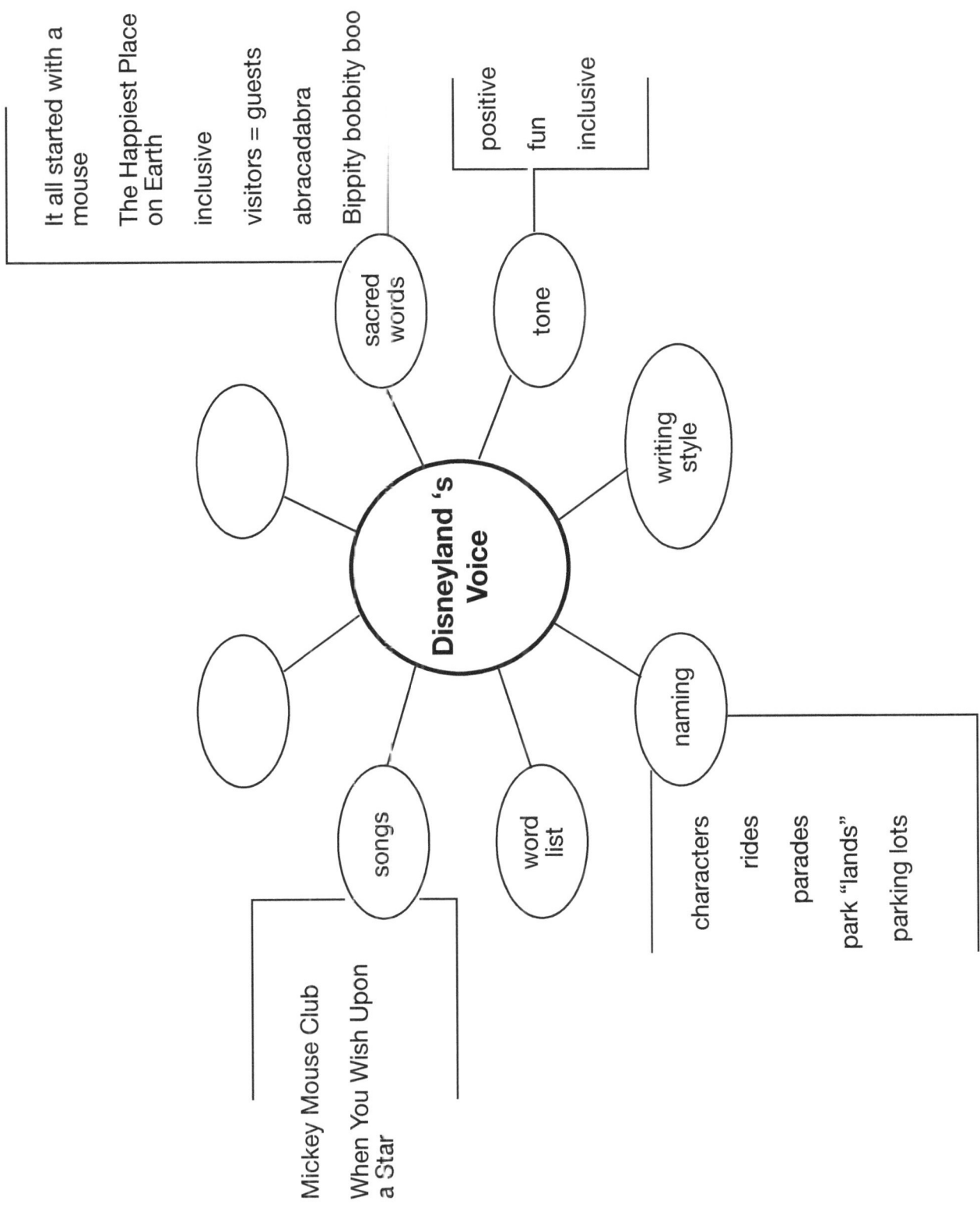

Disneyland 's Voice

sacred words
- It all started with a mouse
- The Happiest Place on Earth
- inclusive
- visitors = guests
- abracadabra
- Bippity bobbity boo

tone
- positive
- fun
- inclusive

writing style

naming
- characters
- rides
- parades
- park "lands"
- parking lots

word list

songs
- Mickey Mouse Club
- When You Wish Upon a Star

Notes and Ideas

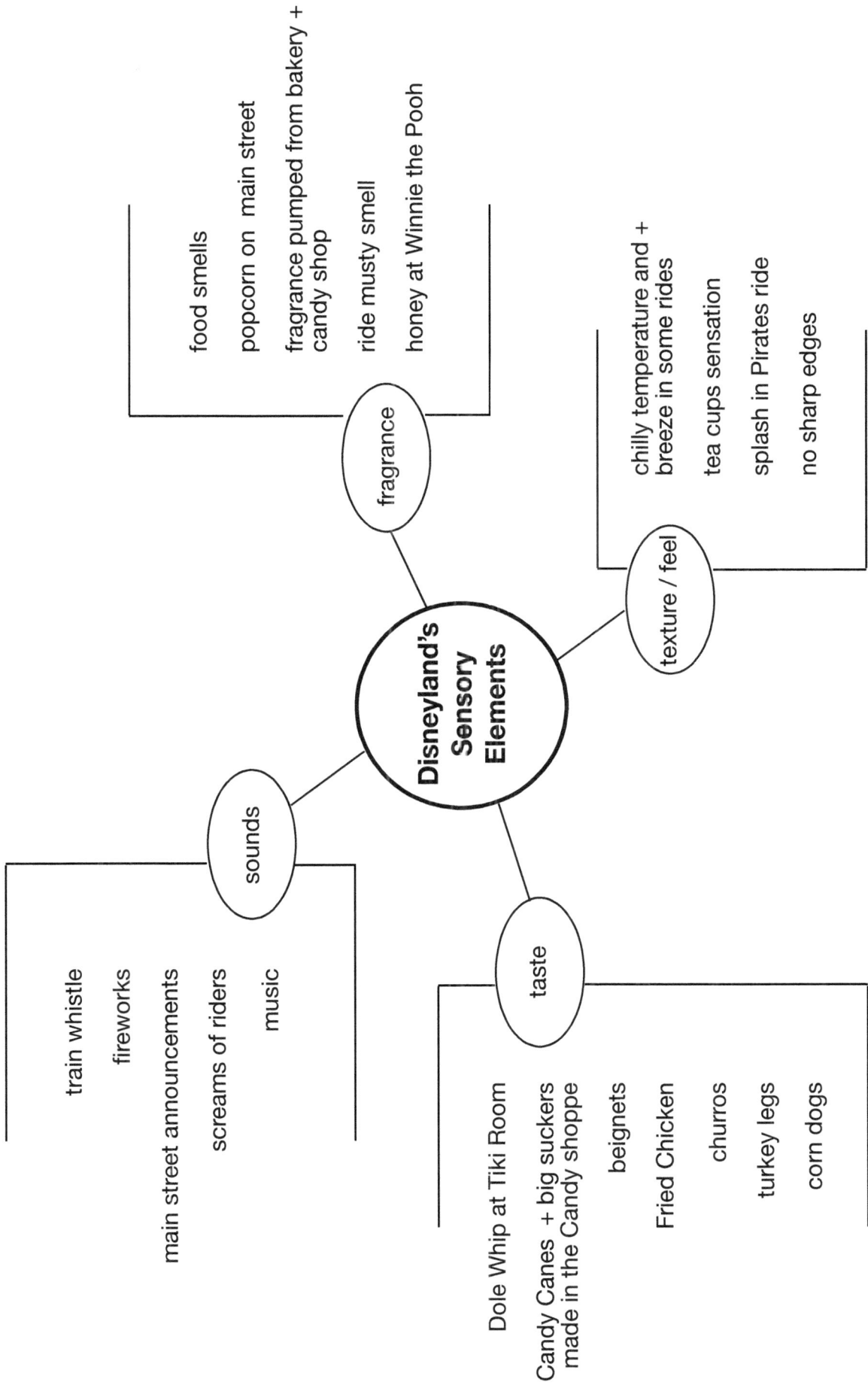

Disneyland's Sensory Elements

fragrance
- food smells
- popcorn on main street
- fragrance pumped from bakery + candy shop
- ride musty smell
- honey at Winnie the Pooh

texture / feel
- chilly temperature and + breeze in some rides
- tea cups sensation
- splash in Pirates ride
- no sharp edges

sounds
- train whistle
- fireworks
- main street announcements
- screams of riders
- music

taste
- Dole Whip at Tiki Room
- Candy Canes + big suckers made in the Candy shoppe
- beignets
- Fried Chicken
- churros
- turkey legs
- corn dogs

Notes and Ideas

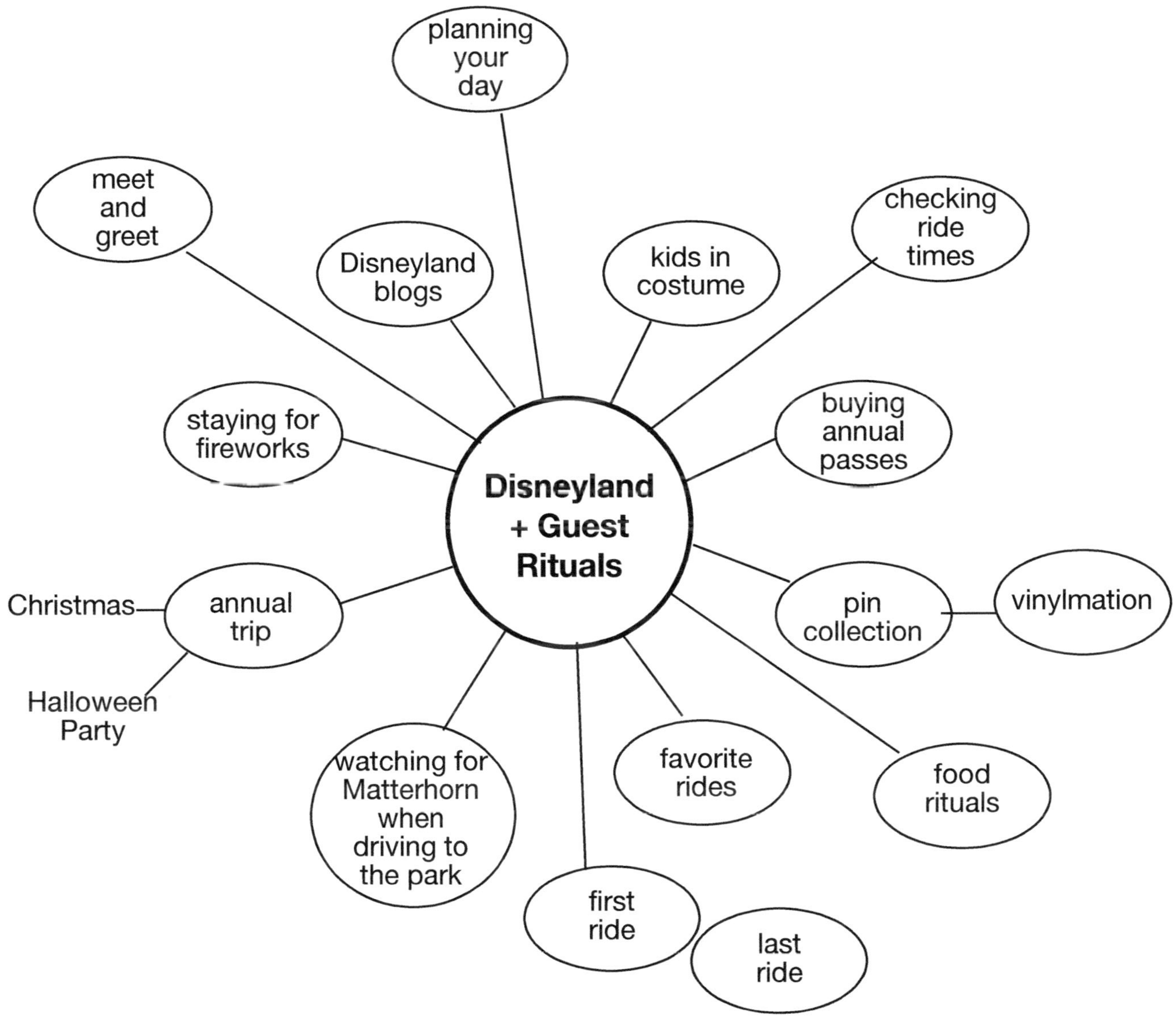
Disneyland + Guest Rituals
planning your day
meet and greet
Disneyland blogs
kids in costume
checking ride times
staying for fireworks
buying annual passes
annual trip
Christmas
Halloween Party
pin collection
vinylmation
watching for Matterhorn when driving to the park
favorite rides
food rituals
first ride
last ride

Notes and Ideas

What Disneyland Does to Delight

hide the seams
- night time maintenance
- cleanup is priority
- keeping all in good repair
- cast members are never seen arriving
- no two of any character at same time
- foliage and artwork hiding construction
- don't break the magic

living our values
- treating guests with respect
- making experiences that can be enjoyed by both children and adults.
- accommodate disabled
- accommodate multiple languages
- accommodate dietary restrictions

honor history
- Lincoln animatronic
- tree left from original land --the Dominguez tree
- Snow White statues gift
- Lilly Belle train for Walt's wife
- early employees immortalized in random places

holiday theming
- Halloween Party
- Christmas

make everyone feel special
- special treatment for kids
- accommodations for disabled
- special diets

how we delight
- Tinkerbelle
- surprise music
- music pop-ups
- surprise character visits
- random handouts of balloons and buttons
- virtual Jungle Cruise
- Jungle Cruise script unique to each captain
- little details + hidden jokes
- cast members encouraged to seek out magic moments

Your
UNSTOPPABLE
Brand

Mind Map

Brand Ingredient

Templates

Use the following pages to start working on your brand ingredients. Consider these your starter pages as you may need to use larger pages in order to hold all your ideas.

Notes and Ideas

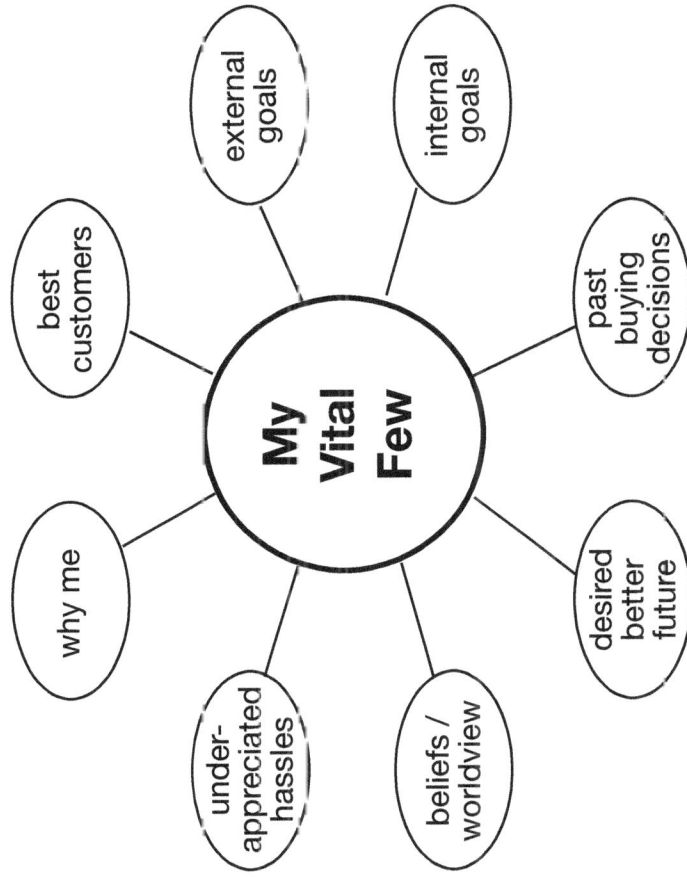

My Vital Few

- best customers
- external goals
- internal goals
- past buying decisions
- desired better future
- beliefs / worldview
- under-appreciated hassles
- why me

Notes and Ideas

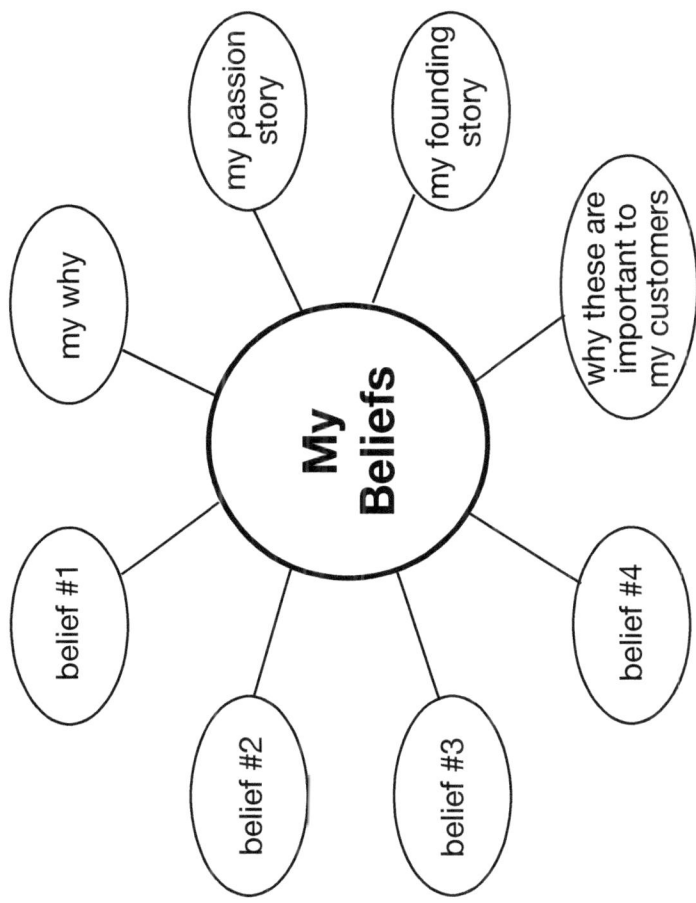

My Beliefs

- my why
- my passion story
- my founding story
- why these are important to my customers
- belief #1
- belief #2
- belief #3
- belief #4

Notes and Ideas

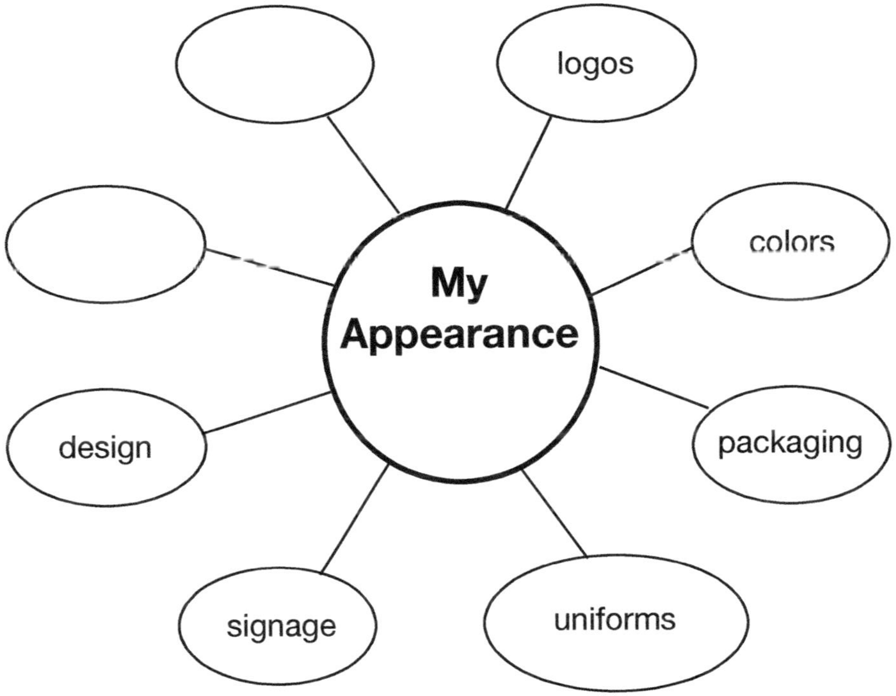
My Appearance
logos
colors
packaging
uniforms
signage
design

Notes and Ideas

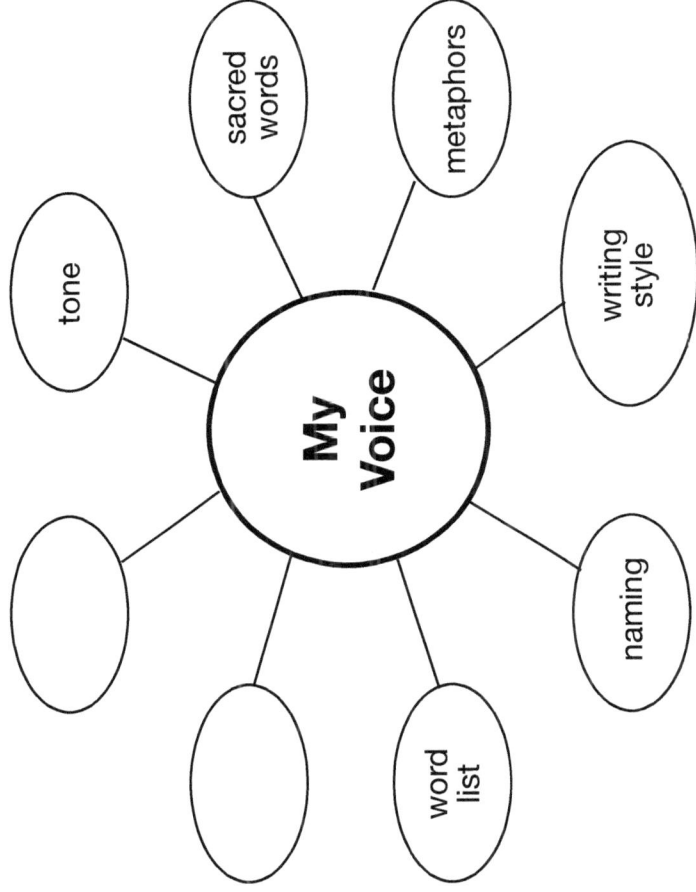

Central circle: **My Voice**

Surrounding ovals:
- tone
- sacred words
- metaphors
- writing style
- naming
- word list
- (blank)
- (blank)

Notes and Ideas

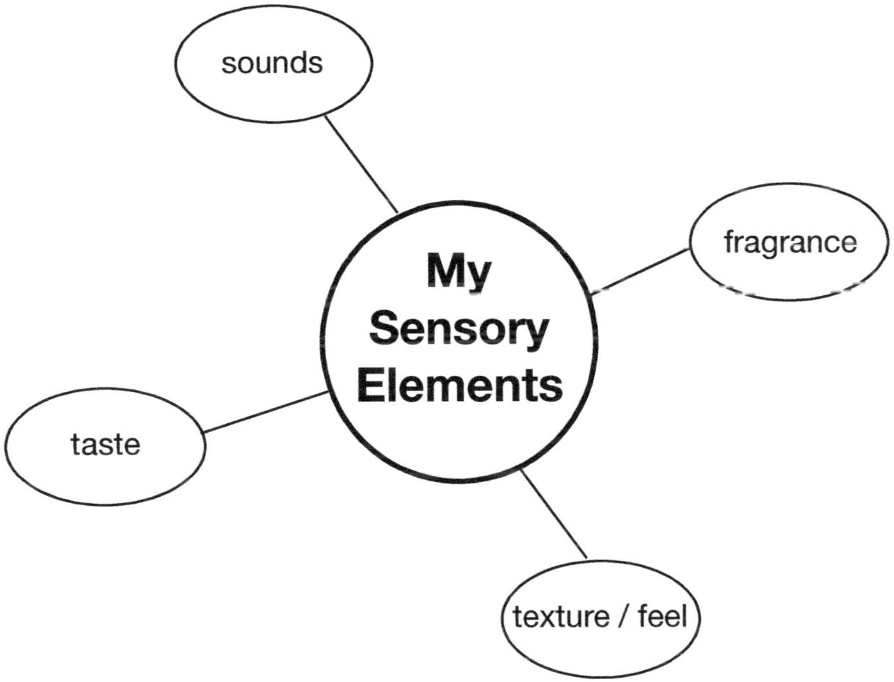
sounds
fragrance
My Sensory Elements
taste
texture / feel

Notes and Ideas

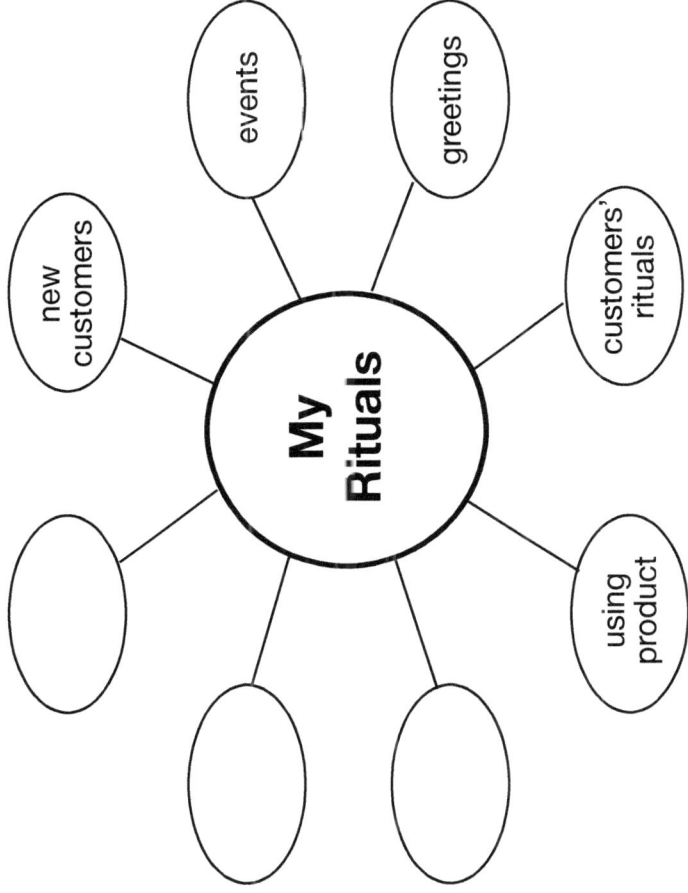

My Rituals

- new customers
- events
- greetings
- customers' rituals
- using product

Notes and Ideas

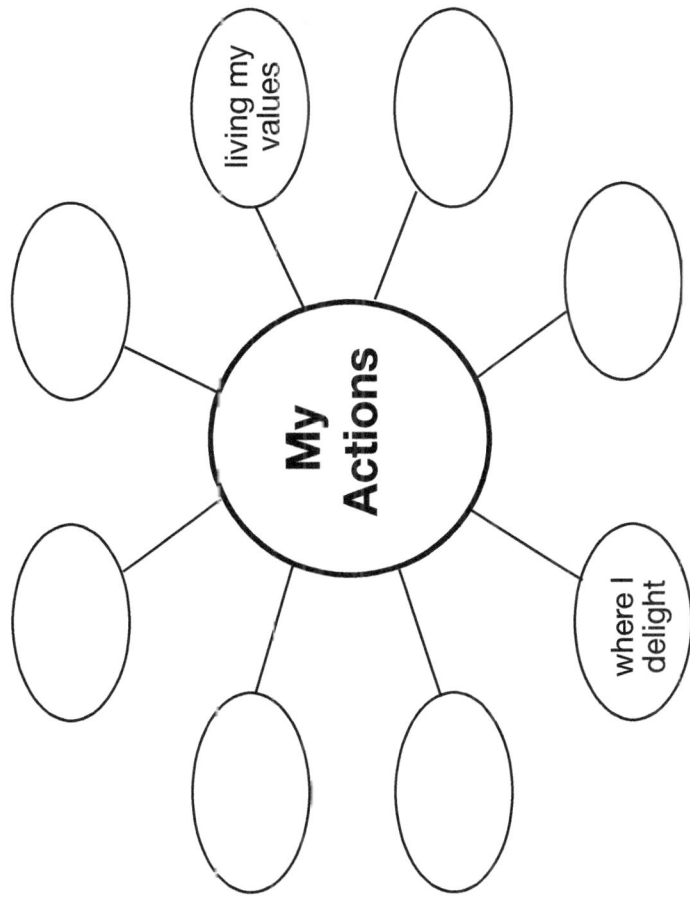

My Actions

living my values

where I delight

My Action Items

THE FLAVOR OF YOUR BRAND

What About Flavor?

And so we arrive at the end of our journey and I want to leave you with some parting thoughts on brand and flavor. My hope is to inspire you to think beyond just those elements on your mindmaps. I want you to see your brand recipe as more than just the ingredients, tools and instructions.

And, I want to leave you with a tool that will help you stay the course with your brand recipe and allow you to share what you have created with others, be they employees, vendors, service providers, or partners.

Focus on the Whole, Not the Parts.

After all, what is the point of all this work if your recipe does have create spectacular flavor?

When a master chef creates a luscious new dish, he is focused on the desired end result—how the finished product is more than the sum of its individual parts. It is elevated. It is sublime. Anyone can throw together some ingredients and make a dish that is edible. Maybe even tasty. But it takes an artistic chef to create a masterpiece.

And so it is with brands. Just filling out the mindmaps and doing a grab bag of "things" may work for you, but it is only when you move beyond the basics that you start to see extraordinary results. This happens when the individual items work together to create something special.

You don't notice the peanut butter or chocolate in the chili as distinct flavors. You just know it is the best chili you have ever eaten and there is something special about it. You create pairings of old favorites, like cinnamon and apple, and new ones like avocado and chocolate to create flavors that are better than the individual components.

Think of Your Brand as a Flavor

Notice in our recipe we talked about creating a feeling. An emotional connection with our customers.

And we talked about creating that feeling through specific actions taken intentionally and consistently. We talked about creating stories as a way to deliver that feeling in your customer's mind.

You may never have thought of flavor and brand and story as being connected.

But now is the time to think of your brand as a flavor.

Flavor is the end result of our recipe.

Just as each of us has a unique reaction to food flavors, we each have unique reactions to brands. Our goal is to create the flavor most appealing to our target audience.

We think of flavor as a tangible thing. After all, it requires molecules to coat our tongues and waft into our nasal passages and then disappears into our minds. Stories are similar. They start with words or images that tell the story but the reality is the story happens in our brains. We can also make our own stories seemingly from nothing. But they aren't from nothing are they? They are the result of our thoughts, our desires, our experiences, our biases, our dreams.

What is the most important link between flavor, brand and story?

Flavor, brand and story are created in the mind. Flavors are not just taste since taste is only sweet, salty, sour, bitter, and umami (savory). Taste is created in the mouth.

Flavor also includes smell. This is the aroma of the volatile molecules that rise from the substance and enter our noses. Smell is far more important to our sensation of flavor than taste. Anyone who has ever said, "If coffee could taste as great as it smells, I would love it!" knows this. Coffee's flavor is a combination of the aroma plus the bitter taste. Without the aroma, all you have is bitter. Which does lead to the question why do they put those plastic lids on coffee with just the small hole to drink and stop the aroma from reaching our noses? And even more importantly, why hasn't one of these modern sensory experts fixed this problem? But I digress.

The totality of flavor, what we are thinking of when we anticipate that onion soup, or luscious chocolate cake or your mom's meatloaf is formed in the mind. This is where the taste (from the mouth) plus the aroma (from the nose) plus your genetics, expectations, memories, experiences, and preferences all combine to make your unique flavor perception.

Without the mind getting involved, we would all have the same response to every food. We would all love oysters, and okra and cilantro and kimchi. But anyone trying to make a meal for a group knows how difficult it is to please everyone. So you can't use cheese because Uncle Jim won't eat cheese. Aunt Bertha always complains that the food doesn't have enough salt. But Jerry wants lots of butter while Susie won't touch tomatoes. We are forced to customize our desired meal plan to fit the unique flavors each guest will create from the food placed before them.

All of this may seem obvious. But is it as obvious that the same thing goes on with branding and story?

Your Brand Attracts Your Best Customer

When you write a customer story, your founding story or product stories, do you expect everyone to have the same reaction? We often don't think about that. We are busy writing the story we want to tell. We also want it to appeal to everyone thinking this will create more buyers.

But a *Recipe for Sticky Customers* helps you design a flavor that appeals only to your desired audience. You can't create a recipe that has universal appeal. Heck, not even chocolate has universal appeal. But the more you focus on your desired flavor the more appealing it will be to those who love you.

Why bother with the whole flavor-equals-brand idea? Doesn't that just complicate things? Why not just focus on the elements you defined earlier and forget all this flavor is brand stuff?

Because just as creative pairing of food ingredients can create exciting new flavor experiences, creative use of your branding elements creates exciting new emotional connections with your customers. Your brand elements are no longer individual things you do. They are part of a great whole. The surprising alchemy is in the way they combine and then excite your customers. Just like avocado in your secret brownie recipe.

The Flavor Wheel

You may be a bit overwhelmed with all the ideas you have and the mindmaps you have created. Even here, the world of flavor analysis can help.

Ever wonder how people come up with wine terms like cut grass, leather, rotten egg, rubber, nail polish remover? Most people would never come up with words like this on their own. Give someone a glass of wine and they may recognize aromas but can't quite find the words. This is natural phenomenon. That is why the flavor wheel was devised.

The flavor wheel gives people a common language to use and allows us to identify those elusive flavor names. When doing sensory testing, everyone is using the same wheel to help the tasters with a reliable, objective classification system.

Create Your Flavor Wheel

Your Brand Flavor Wheel is a handy visual that everyone who touches your brand can use. You, employees, contractors, designers, and writers can use this to have the same language. It puts the important aspects of your brand flavor in one handy visual.

Use it every time to write a blog post, create an ad, design a promotion. This Flavor Wheel is what keeps your grounded and attached to your target audience. It is who you are as a business.

For ideas on flavor wheels just do a Pinterest search to see a wide variety of flavor wheels for coffee, wine, beer, cheese salami. Pick a favorite food and check out a wheel that interests you.

For background information on favor wheels, go to:

https://www.escoffieronline.com/the-essence-of-food-understanding-the-flavor-wheel-infographic/

Creating Your Flavor Wheel

The wheel is separated into four categories. Your audience, your beliefs, your story triggers and customer touch points.

In Audience, refer to your Vital Few mindmap, especially the external goals, the internal goals and the world views identified.

In Shared Beliefs, list the beliefs you share with your audience. These are beliefs that help define your tribe and make strong emotional connections.

In Story Triggers, identify words that will trigger the right stories in the mind of your reader and images that will do the same.

In Customer Touch Points list places (email, web site, packaging, workshops,etc.) that have the most power to connect with your desired customer. Also include unusual places that might help you stand out.

Your Brand Favor Wheel

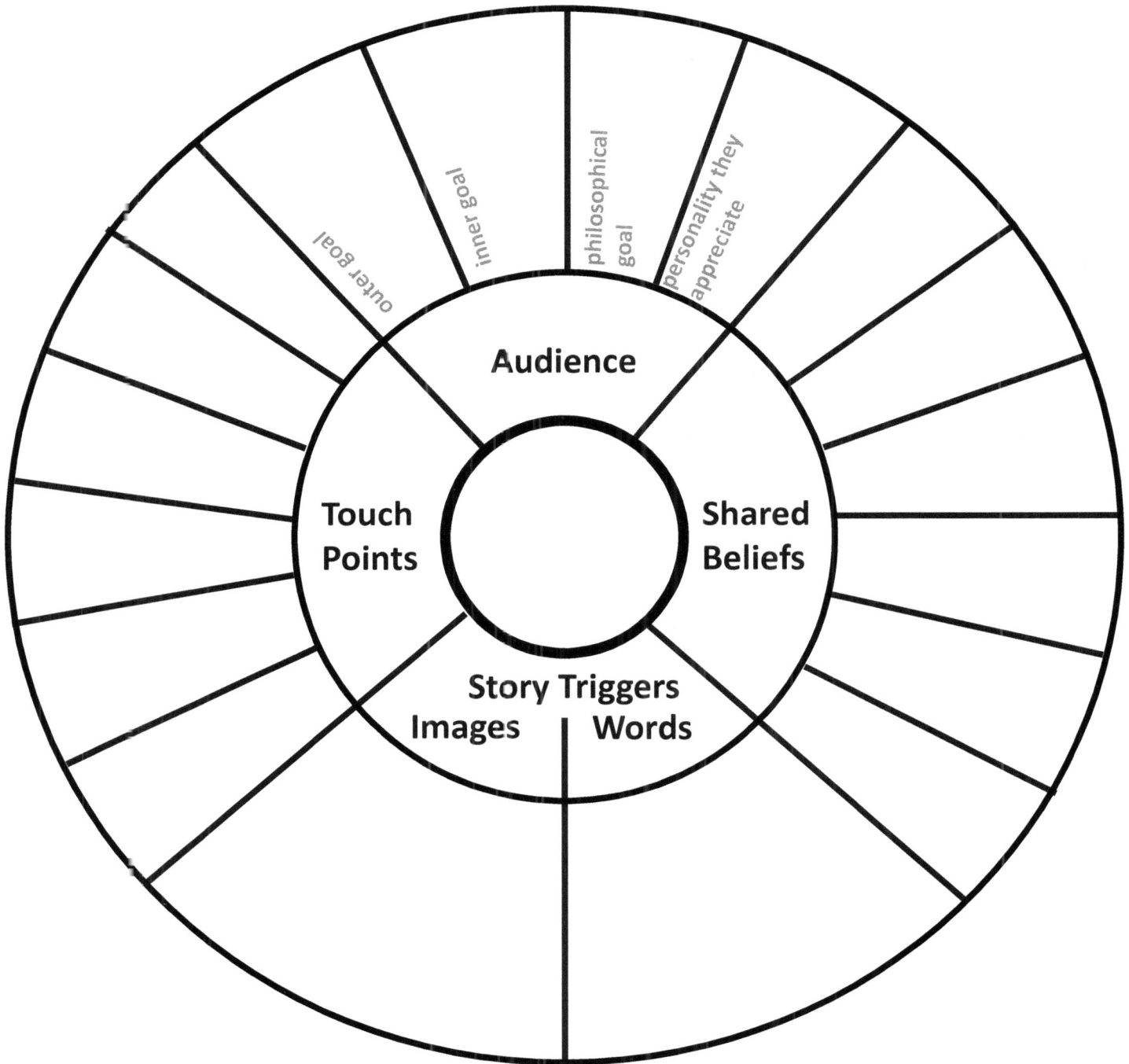

Audience

outer goal

inner goal

philosophical goal

personality they appreciate

Touch Points

Shared Beliefs

Story Triggers

Images

Words

Books

The Business of Belief by Tom Asacker

Primal Branding: Create Zealots for Your Brand, Your Company, and Your Future by Patrick Hanlon

StoryBranding: Creating Standout Brands through the Power of Story by Jim Signorelli

StorySmart: Using the Science of Story to Persuade, Influence, Inspire and Teach by Kendall Haven

Whoever Tells the Best Story Wins: How to Use Your Own Stories to Communicate with Power and Impact by Annette Simmons

Words That Work: It's Not What You Say. It's What People Hear by Dr. Frank Luntz

Words That Sell by Richard Bayan

Example Letter from a Customer
https://code.likeagirl.io/i-am-a-woman-in-tech-and-this-is-what-i-want-in-a-company-f6177569a287

Example of Sticky Branding
www.monstersupplies.org (for backstory on this retail arm of a nonprofit read: https://www.dan-dad.org/en/d-ad-hoxton-street-monster-supplies-case-study-insights/

Video Series on Branding + Story
www.storybrand.com: Avoid the marketing money pit: http://storybrand.com/marketing-plan-made-easy/ (just watch the four free videos at the top of the page). Great resource on branding, storytelling and creating a clear message for your customers.

Cost Free, Royalty Free Images
Unsplash
Pixabay
Freestock
Freerangestock